DATE DUE

Other Borzoi Books for Young People
by Cornelia Spencer

MADE IN INDIA

The story of India's people and of their gifts to the world
Illustrated by Allen Lewis and with photographs

MADE IN CHINA

The story of China's expression
Foreword by Lin Yutang
Illustrated by Kurt Wiese and with photographs

Made in Japan

"The arts of the Japanese people have attracted the world for hundreds of years because they have a quality all their own—a quality that is hard to capture and almost impossible to describe. These island people bring their love of beauty into everyday life perhaps more than any other people in the world. Their houses, gardens, furniture, utensils, and fabrics all show their inborn sense of form and color. A woman who comes to sell a few freshly caught fish at your door shows her feeling for design in the way she arranges them so beautifully upon leaves in her flat basket. Courtesy between members of a family and respect for each person in the community express beauty in terms of human relationships as among no other people. Gestures, smiles, and murmured words of politeness all suggest that each individual is important.

"These are the people whose country and whose personality have given the world many treasures."—*from the Foreword*

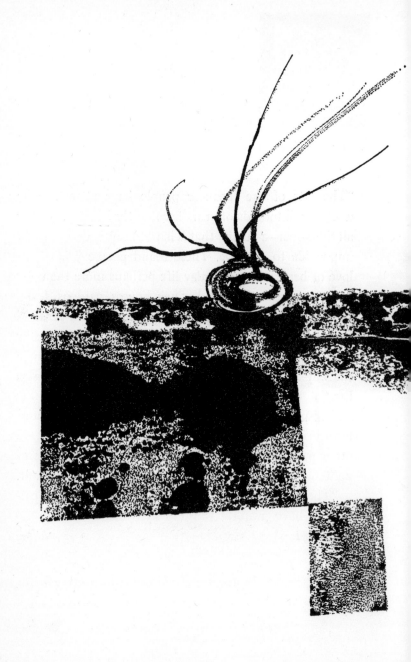

Made in Japan

BY CORNELIA SPENCER

Illustrated by Richard Powers and with photographs

ALFRED A. KNOPF · NEW YORK

Grateful acknowledgement is made
for permission to use the following photographs:

Library of Congress
     1, 24

Metropolitan Museum of Art
     Rogers Fund, 1919.   20
     Howard Mansfield Collection, Rogers Fund, 1936.   21
     Fletcher Fund, 1929.   23

The Smithsonian Institution, Freer Gallery of Art
     7, 8, 9, 10, 11, 12, 13, 14, 15, 16,
     17, 18, 19, 22, 25, 26, 27, 28

Tokyo National Museum
     2, 3, 4, 6

12-11-63

L. C. catalog card number: 63-9108

THIS IS A BORZOI BOOK, PUBLISHED BY ALFRED A. KNOPF, INC.

Contents

Made in Japan

A Foreword

The arts of the Japanese people have attracted the world for hundreds of years because they have a quality all their own—a quality that is hard to capture and almost impossible to describe.

The major theme of Japan's art is people rather than nature; people, instead of the rain beating down on their paper umbrellas; people, and not the swirling snow itself though it blinds them as they work on the mountainside; boatmen, rather than the gale that is billowing the sails of their tiny craft, tipping it dangerously in heavy seas. Japanese art is about people because the Japanese are realistic and down-to-earth, not philosophers like the Chinese nor poets like the Indians. They take life as it comes and make the best of it, and they do not spend much time discussing abstract theories about its meaning, though they may stand completely enchanted by the sudden glimpses of a foaming waterfall or a vista of pink cherry blossoms or of Mount Fuji, their sacred mountain, rising above the clouds shrouded in rain or glistening white against an azure sky. This peak appears and reappears in many forms in their arts, symbolizing the fact that nature is beyond their control.

Japanese art has strength and personality, which is not surprising if one thinks about the country. A chain of volcanic islands whipped by winds and washed by breakers and tidal waves, often battered by typhoons or shaken by earthquakes, Japan is at the mercy of nature's whims. The sea is her master, for it surrounds her and divides her by many inland channels and invades even wooded reaches in her unexpected bays and inlets.

The amount of arable land is small, only fifteen per cent of the total land area of 150,000 square miles, and the people work every foot of it with enormous energy. When the land has given all it can, there are still the products of the sea to be harvested. Fish, shellfish, and even ocean plants are staples in the Japanese diet; they are also important exports. Hard work, ingenuity, and great determination make survival possible.

Although they have to struggle to live, these island people bring their love of beauty into everyday life perhaps more than any other people. Their houses, gardens, furniture, utensils, and fabrics all show their inborn sense of color and form. A woman who comes to sell a few freshly caught fish at your door must have a feeling for design to lay them so beautifully upon leaves in her flat basket. Courtesy between members of a family and respect for each person in the community express beauty in terms of human relationships as among no other people. Gestures, smiles, and murmured words of politeness all suggest that each individual is important.

These are the people whose country and whose personality have given the world many treasures.

1

The Backdrop of History

The first people to live in Japan were probably relatives of the Eskimos and the American Indians. We know that Russia was once connected with Alaska, and that the Japanese islands were very likely joined to the Asian mainland at one time. The white-skinned Ainu who still live in some parts of Japan are remnants of these early people.

The Japanese themselves say that their beginnings abounded in magic and miracle. A pair called Izanagi and Izanami were the most important individuals. Izanagi dipped his magic spear into the ocean one day; as he lifted it out, drops falling from it formed the islands that became Japan. This was only the start of a long period during which thousands of gods were born in all sorts of ways. They were spirits of mountains and streams, waterfalls and rocks, and gradually grew into gods and goddesses who were patrons of villages and then were claimed as the ancestors of later clans.

The first ruler of Japan to step out of myth and shake off his trailing clouds of fable was Emperor Jimmu, or Heavenly Emperor, who was born on the largest island, Kyushu, about 660 B.C. Marching eastward, he organized several tribes on the northern shore of the Inland Sea. These he governed from a center in Yamato, the province where the city of Nara now stands.

Asuka (Korean) Period
300–645 A.D.

During the next few centuries the Chinese Han dynasty was reigning brilliantly on the mainland to the west. When it lost its power at the beginning of the third century A.D., the men of Yamato undertook their first great adventure. They crossed the water to the mainland and Korea. There is a legend that these were not the first Japanese to reach this country. An Empress Jingo, who did not belong to the Yamato royal line, is said to have led an expedition there in 200 A.D.

The Koreans had long been oppressed by the Chinese and now they were busy getting back all they could by looting the Han capital, Loyang. When the daring Japanese invaders from Yamato offered to help them, they were delighted. The Koreans even sent envoys with gifts to the Japanese court and begged further help against the Chinese. Gifts of jade beads, bronze mirrors, iron swords, images of Buddha, and copies of Indian Buddhist scriptures astounded the leaders at Yamato. They had not known that such things existed. Some of the Korean envoys were musicians or doctors. Some knew how to devise calendars.

Koreans were not the only visitors Japan received as time passed, although they had the strongest influence on her life for a hundred years or more. During this time immigrants from China and perhaps from islands of the South Pacific arrived. Chinese and Korean refugees from the mainland were given land and excused from taxes because of all they could teach the less advanced Japanese.

The most important thing these immigrants taught was the Buddhist religion. When Buddhism reached Japan in 552, the people were at first afraid that it might anger the nature gods whom they revered in the early form of Shinto, the Japanese national religion. But they could not resist what Buddhism could give; for it offered not only a religious practice but also well-developed sculpture, architecture, painting, and a written language. It was a rich new world of culture and beauty unlike anything the simple people of the islands had known before.

A powerful family named Soga championed Buddhism and won the throne in 593 under Empress Suiko. Prince Shotoku, son of the former emperor, was really heir to this position and was recognized as such even though he had sided with the Soga family on the question of Buddhism. Though he never actually reigned, he influenced the Japanese in their feeling about the new religion a great deal. When he accepted the faith about the year 600 A.D. this ended their hesitancy toward it. Japan now began to use a written language for the first time. Histories, the *Kojiki* and the *Nihonji*, and books of poems all written in Chinese, became important at the Japanese court long before there was writing in Japanese. Prince Shotoku was interested in learning about China; so when affairs there settled down under the new Sui dynasty, he sent envoys across to the mainland.

Because the envoys did not return until the T'ang dynasty, famous for its brilliance, had replaced the Sui, the prince to whom they hoped to report was already dead. Kamatari, a young man of the Yamato line, and a brother (Karu) as well as a son (Prince Naka) of the reigning emperor had seized control of the government. The young men determined to pattern the Japanese government on that of China and hoped to see a permanent capital built for it. They did not step out as leaders but worked through others, although Karu set up a reign called Taikwa in which many reforms were begun. Prince Naka followed him as Emperor Tenchi, but was on the throne only ten years. His envoys to the T'ang court in China asked that their country from that time on be known as Nippon, or Sunrise Land, instead of Yamato. Emperor Tenchi became famous for the important organization of laws known as the Taiho Code.

Kamatari had done a great deal for the people. He was rewarded with the gift of large estates in the Fujiwara district of Yamato. Kamatari here founded the Fujiwara family, Japan's most important family, which much later gave its name to a period of her history. One of the most brilliant ages of her arts is called the

Fujiwara and many outstanding businesses have carried this name down through the years. The Fujiwara family was sometimes more powerful than the court itself.

Emperor Temmu, who followed Emperor Tenchi, set up his capital at Asuka, giving the period its name. He made it as Chinese as he could, but this did not satisfy him. He dreamed of a new city patterned after Sian, the capital of the T'ang emperors. It would be located at Nara.

Nara (Chinese) Period
645–794 A.D.

Nara was the first real capital of Japan. Until this time the governing center had been moved about in the provinces. Even Emperor Tenchi's palace had been no more than a log building without the bark removed, but Nara was a Chinese city. When it was completed in 710, during the reign of Empress Gemmyo, the Yamato court moved there. All the pains that the artisans had taken in choosing each stone and smoothing every beam seemed justified. Buddhist temples and government buildings breathed beauty and prestige. Anything that was not in keeping was rejected. State ceremonies, religious festivals, and everyday events followed Chinese traditions. The government itself was based on that of China.

In literature, too, China was the teacher. Many of the people of the Nara court took literature seriously. *Manyoshu*, a collection of poems by more than six hundred writers, was completed. Some of the poems were rituals, some were lyrics composed by students who had visited China. Students and priests continued to go to the T'ang court to learn more.

Finding a way of writing Japanese had never seemed important until this time. If writing was needed, Chinese characters had been used. But the people were now no longer satisfied to have their stories and fables preserved only by memorizing them. They demanded written Japanese. This demand was hard to satisfy. Chinese characters were pulled and twisted to give either the sound or the meaning of Japanese words. The result was most confusing. Between the years 600 and 800 A.D., the Japanese did succeed in constructing a kind of written language; but it was still closely connected with the Chinese and would remain so. Even today Japanese is one of the most difficult written languages of the world.

As the Japanese came to have a stronger national feeling, it irked them to live under the authority of Buddhist groups which they had welcomed earlier, because of what they could teach. Friction grew between the powerful Fujiwara clan and the Buddhist priests. The Fujiwara at last succeeded in asserting itself as the imperial family through Kwammu, who was emperor from 782 to 805 A.D.

Early Heian (Kyoto) Period: The Fujiwara 794–894

Emperor Kwammu moved the capital from Nara to Kyoto, which was then called Heian, in 794. This period is known as the Heian or the Fujiwara after either the capital city or the leading group.

One important reason why Emperor Kwammu changed the center of his government was that Buddhist monks had become too powerful in Nara. One ambitious one had threatened to seize the throne. The emperor did not want to abandon Buddhist culture. He authorized and encouraged the building of new temples and was glad to accept the help of two young priests, Saicho and Kukai, who were gifted artists.

The Fujiwara were prospering; but they knew that to remain powerful they needed to be unified. They did all they could to draw together the members of their family. They stressed ancestor worship; they married their daughters into the imperial family whenever it was possible; they missed no chance to serve the emperor so that he would be under obligation to reward them with important positions. Anyone who got in their way was in danger of demotion or even of execution on some pretext or other. The emperor had to do what the Fujiwara family wanted. The court grew refined, beautiful, and rich under the guidance and authority of the clan.

Late Heian (Kyoto): The Fujiwara 894–1185 A.D.

The Fujiwara had to struggle to keep their power. The comfortable, gracious life at court was supported precariously. They had managed to get title to most of the best farmlands as time passed, and they collected heavy taxes from these to finance the court. Some provincial landlords grew angry about the taxes imposed on them and hired warriors to protect their holdings from unfair practices and from seizure. Two of these landlord families were the important Taira and Minamoto.

Opposition to the Fujiwara increased steadily. Temples began to notice that contributions toward their upkeep were becoming smaller than they had been. Protesting monks armed themselves and even went to attack the capital. The Taira and Minamoto clansmen came to be rivals over which line the next emperor should come from, for both families could claim imperial descent.

Kamakura Period: Age of Military Dictators 1185–1338

When Yorimoto succeeded to the leadership of the Minamoto clan, he was accepted even by the Taira family because of his ability. He was a key figure in history because he gradually drew the power of the government away from Heian to the fishing village of Kamakura, where he set up a military dictatorship. This was a *shogunate* and he was the *shogun*. Japan now really had two capitals; for the imperial court was still in Heian and the military ruler governed from Kamakura. Though Yorimoto did not set up a dynasty he brought much more of Japan under his military rule than had ever been under the throne. He began a new period of history under military leaders which lasted for seven hundred years. It brought great cultural advances.

After Yorimoto's death in 1199, regents of the Hojo family, to which his wife belonged, were in power. Things changed. Buddhism which had been a rich, comforting religion became a gloomy, ascetic, severe way of life. Priests often living in bare, chilly monasteries warned that Japan was facing hard times, and one of them even foretold that Mongols from the mainland would one day attack her.

Japanese pirates had kept on bothering the coasts of Korea and China for a long time. Now the great Kublai Khan was at the head of the Mongol dynasty in China and he decided to stop the pirates once and for all by invading Japan itself. Such a plan did not seem too wild; the Mongol court was fantastically rich, and the Khan's empire stretched from the Persian Gulf to the China Sea. Marco Polo, who was carrying out expeditions for the Khan, later referred in his book of travels, to the large island of "Zepangu," whose "inhabitants, though living quite separate from other nations, are fair, handsome, and of agreeable manner."

Two Mongol attacks made with thousands of ships, first in 1271 and then ten years later, were repulsed by the Japanese. These defeats were partly due to terrible storms which arose at the crucial moment and broke the invading ships to pieces.

Though the invasions had failed, the strongly military atmosphere of the Japanese court was affected by the fact that they had been attempted. The leaders there emphasized military power more than ever. Military standing came to be the only real measure of one's social position. The "Way of the Sword," or the cult of *Bushido*, was idealized. Bravery developed as a characteristic of the Japanese people. Honor might require that a man or even his whole family commit suicide if misfortune came. Swordmaking developed into a fine art and swords have ranked among Japan's art objects since this time. The *samurai*, members of the military nobility, chose cherry blossoms as their symbol because of their simplicity and purity. These qualities stood for a warrior's willingness to give his life for his honor. Sculpture representing a particular hero or an important person and long scrolls picturing a series of events in a man's life became popular. Heroic ballads about the *samurai* were sung to delighted audiences, for it was an age of hero worship.

Ashikaga Shoguns
1338–1565 A.D.

Now a strange state of things came about. Not only did two centers of authority, one in Heian and one in Kamakura, continue, but two governments actually ruled. Heian was claimed by Shogun Ashikaga Takauji as the Northern Court, while the royal emperor escaped to the hills of Yoshino and established the Southern Court there. Then, as soon as the emperor died the Ashikaga *shogun* seized control of both centers.

It was an unhappy period, for there was continual fighting among the military men, who wanted to pull down and destroy the power of the Ashikaga *shoguns*. The last hundred years of the era were marked by actual war.

On the edge of the political struggle an offstage drama was going on with China. By this time the Ming dynasty had replaced that of the Mongols and was busy restoring and beautifying the country which was once more under Chinese rule. But Japanese pirates were still annoying the mainland coast. In order to get control of the situation and save face all around, China allowed a certain number of ships to trade under the sponsorship of Buddhist priests each year, calling them tribute ships. Envoys went back and forth, too, and carried news. In Japan it became the fashion to go down to the shore to see the precious cargoes which arrived from the mainland. *Shogun* Ashikaga Yoshimitsu succeeded in unifying the northern branches of the imperial court in Heian, and the Chinese emperor called him King of Japan.

Under Yoshimitsu many of the arts were encouraged. Music and dancing and the traditional *Noh* plays were popular. Ceremonial tea drinking and landscape gardening, introduced from China during his rule, quickly became fashionable.

Beneath the surface of better times, deep troubles still grew. Those who had become rich through trade with China and those who had to make a living from the land pulled further and further apart. Plague and famine struck. Rivalry between powerful families broke into bitter struggles.

Momoyama (Peach Hill) Period: 1565–1615
The Three Great Dictators

This period was dramatic and important even though it was short. Japan was suddenly brought into the path of world affairs. The western powers were exploring and expanding. Settlers reached North America. The scientific method was growing at a swift rate. European nations were building up their sea power. Portuguese, Spanish, and then Dutch seamen and traders reached Japan. The Jesuit St. Francis Xavier arrived and began to teach Christianity. Even though Japan was going through a confused time, great changes growing out of her contact with the West began.

The Momoyama Period, dominated by three military men of strong personality, was vital and full of vigor. Each of the men was a giant who dreamed of greatness and of building castles to protect himself against the firearms of the foreigners. Each feared and yet was fascinated by the men from across the seas.

The first of the three military dictators was Oda Nobunaga. He built a great castle at Azuchi and there received Portuguese merchants and priests. He found the visitors interesting and made them welcome. He even urged his subjects to accept Christianity and turned against all forms of Buddhism except the sect called Zen. He and his followers liked to practice Zen because it stressed frugality, simplicity, meditation, and ceremonial tea drinking.

Toyotomi Hideyoshi, the second great dictator, had been one of Nobunaga's generals. He was the most colorful of the three, for he had a brilliant mind and was extremely ambitious. He wanted to invade Korea and even attack China. He was a clever organizer, too, for he won over some Buddhists who had been a problem to Nobunaga by getting their help in routing hostile clans. He succeeded in disarming all civilians by asking that all weapons be turned in to provide metal to cast great religious statues. He also instituted a survey of lands so that taxes could be collected more justly. Hideyoshi was interested in the West and sent out envoys to learn more about it. When they returned his household adopted western fashions in food, dress, and amusements. Card games were played, and European books became popular. *Aesop's Fables* was translated into Japanese.

But one day the captain of a shipwrecked Spanish vessel pointed to all the Spanish and Portuguese possessions on a map and told Hideyoshi that Spain and Portugal had taken them by first sending missionaries to make converts of the people. At once the dictator commanded that all missionaries in Japan be executed. Some were crucified, since that seemed to him suitable. Others escaped from Japan, while still others remained to work secretly for their religious beliefs. Hideyoshi himself died a year after he gave the order against the missionaries.

Tokugawa Ieyasu was the third of the great military dictators of the Momoyama Period. He was already middle aged when he came to power, a more seasoned man than those who had gone before him. He wanted to strengthen the country from within and to do this he emphasized mining and agriculture. He realized that a number of dangers threatened. For one thing, China might at any time send an expedition to punish Japan for her collaboration with Korea. For another, ambitious merchants were always ready to turn anything to their personal advantage. The court in Heian was also always a threat to the dictatorship. The Christians who had stayed in the islands were again growing strong.

Ieyasu was interested in Kwanto, an area near Lake Biwa. He decided to establish his government there and centered it in a great castle that had been built there in the previous century. Edo Castle was soon surrounded by the activities of building a city. Plans were laid, and the artisans went to work. Here, as *shogun* of all Japan, Ieyasu set up his dictatorship in what we know as Tokyo.

Although Ieyasu was a military man and ruthless in the measures he used to keep the Tokugawa family line strong, he had many other interests. He encouraged education and the development of literature. He demanded order and good behavior among the people. For a time he did everything he could to keep peace even with the Christians. But when the Christians and others who opposed him took Osaka Castle as their stronghold, he concluded that he would have to destroy it. When it did not fall after a long siege, Ieyasu made truce in a most generous way. This still did not bring the resistance to an end, and he finally attacked the castle and completely defeated those who were opposing him.

Tokugawa or Edo Period: The Closed Door 1615–1867

The problem of Catholics in Japan was not solved even yet. After Ieyasu's death in 1616 they again defied the authority of the acting *shogun*. In 1638 after a bitter seige he rounded them up in the ruined castle of Hara where they had taken refuge and asked Dutch ships to shell the place. In order to avoid this kind of difficulty again, the *shogunate* forbade any kind of contact between Japan and outside countries, with the exception of China. One small port on the island of Deshima in Nagasaki Harbor was kept open to Dutch trade.

This new order started the Closed Door Policy. It lasted for more than two hundred years. Japanese society was carefully organized during this time. Military leaders, nobility, and commoners each had patterns to live by. The Japanese refined their life and developed their arts. Literature, painting, printing by woodblocks, pottery, tapestry, and many other art forms were perfected. The country was prosperous. By the end of the nineteenth century, Tokyo had a population of one million people and was the largest city not only in Japan but in all the world.

When the Tokugawa *shogunate* was overthrown and

Commodore Perry pushed Japan's closed door open in 1853, a new age arrived.

Meiji Period
1867–1912

What is known as the Meiji Restoration began when Emperor Meiji returned to Tokyo from Kyoto or Heian where the royal line had continued for so many years. In Tokyo he assumed control of the country when the last *shogun* resigned.

The new age was the most epoch-making in all Japan's history up to 1912. Japan patterned her military power after that of the West, set up factories, and studied the ways of the western world. Foreigners came to the islands and Japanese students fanned out in all directions. An enormous exchange of information and culture began.

Until now Japan had looked toward China for guidance in the arts. Now China was forgotten, for Japan rejected what had been traditional and eagerly pursued whatever was new. The effect on her arts was startling.

Most startling of all was the impact of western science and technology. These became available to thousands of students because the new Ministry of Education established universal education and modern colleges. Nationalism blossomed as Japan became modernized. Seeing that colonization was carried on successfully by other powers, Japan dreamed of expanding. Compulsory military service became a law. Before many years had passed the Japanese army was finding new areas where a crowded population might spread. By the end of the First World War Japan was one of the great powers. When the Second World War came she was ready to grasp control of Asia. The results of that attempt are modern history.

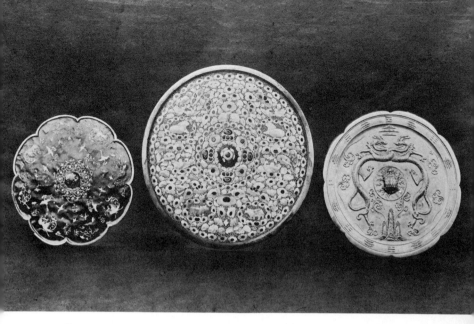

1: Bronze mirrors, from the Grave Mound Period and later.

2: A clay haniwa, from the Grave Mound Period. A man and a woman dancer.

3: A *clay* haniwa *armored warrior, from the Grave Mound
    Period.*

4: A *clay* haniwa *wild boar, from the Grave Mound Period.*

5: *Main shrine of Naikū Kōtaijingū. The inner shrine at
    Ise.*

6: *Jomon clay figurine.*

7: *Owari shino pottery tea bowl—late 19th century.*

8: *Raku pottery by Koetsu. Momoyama Period (1558–1637), Kyoto.*

9: *Karatsu pottery (Chosengaratsu), named for port town for Korea.*

10: *Imari pottery plate in several colors. 1700 A.D. (21 13/16 inches in diameter).*

11: *Octagonal pottery dish, Kakiemon. Early 18th century. Fish and water plants, in clear colors.*

12: *Lacquer chest of drawers. 18th century (8⅛ by 6⅝ inches).*

13: *Bodhisattva of wood, covered with lacquer and gilt. Suiko Period (A.D. 552–645) 37 11/16 inches.*

14: *Guardian figure of wood, Kamakura period (1185–1392) 7 feet 2 inches high.*

15: *Winter: young woman in snow. Painting on silk. Genre School (Ukiyo-e). Koryusai (1764–1780).*

16: *Winter landscape. Kano School. Hogai (1828–1888).*

17: *Three monkeys and flowers. Painting on silk. Sosen, Mori (1749–1821).*

18: *An actor—a silk panel. Genre School (Ukiyo-e). Shunko, Katsukawa.*

19: *"Mount Fuji," ink and colors on silk. Hokusai, Katsushika (1760–1849).*

24: *"Shower at Shono," from "The Fifty-three Stages of the Tokaido," by Hiroshige.*

25: *Mimosa trees and flowers, four-fold screen of paper by Sosetsu. Momoyana Decorative School.*

26: *Snow-laden cryptomeria and cedar trees. Six-fold screen of paper. Kano School, Momoyama Period.*

27: *Waves at Matsushima. Six-fold screen of paper by Sotatsu, Momoyama Period.*

28: *"Tuning the Samisen," ink on paper drawing by Hokusai
(1760–1849).*

2

Houses of Men and Gods

Which can tell us more about the Japanese; their homes or their temples? If their houses show a love of beauty as clearly as their great temples, must we not believe that their feeling for what is lovely simply will not be suppressed? Although a farmhouse may be very different from a city shrine, we will find an artistic touch in both.

We can get some idea of the earliest Japanese homes from actual ruins, from pictures, and from models. The ruins are shell mounds and remains of pit houses. Mounds of shells in some places near the coast mark locations where Late Stone Age families must have lived. They seem to have found shelter in caves or under overhanging rocks while they hunted or fished. The shells which they discarded after eating oysters, clams, or other shellfish piled up around the places where they lived and marked them for archaeologists who would come centuries later.

The people of the shell mounds were probably ancestors of the Ainu tribes of Japan and came from the same Caucasian roots as people of northern Europe and Asia. Theirs were the earliest homesites of Japan.

Pit houses of the next period were dug or scraped out of the ground and then covered with a simple roof of limbs, leafy branches, or grass. Marks of these houses can still be seen, usually clustered near sources of fresh water. They had their good points, for they nestled close to the earth and so were quite warm. They were easy to build; therefore, in case of danger or epidemic, their owners could abandon them. The floor of a pit house was usually a square or semicircle of pounded earth. Sometimes it had a hearth lined with stones. At some sites one can still see sockets for the posts that once supported the roof. Ruins of pit houses are found in the northern part of the islands where the climate is fairly dry and heavy rains or sudden storms are unlikely.

Pit houses led to the most familiar kind of Japanese house. As time passed, the roof of limbs was raised higher and higher. Two posts set in the ground supported a ridgepole, and pairs of rafters which reached to the ground were lashed slantwise to each end of the pole. Horizontal beams were then tied in place on the sloping sides formed by the rafters to make a framework for thatch. The thatch served as both roof and wall, like the sides of a tent. Later the roof itself was raised as vertical wooden walls were added beneath it. Wooden floors sometimes replaced the scraped or pounded earth. The pit house had evolved into the Japanese house.

Objects picturing the houses which followed the pit houses have been found in grave mounds of the third to the sixth century A.D. Treasures made of bronze, precious stones, and pottery were put in the tombs of leading men. Even though bronze itself first came from China by way of Korea, some of the pieces in the grave mounds were decorated with Japanese designs. Polished metal mirrors and strange bells or *dotaku* were incised with line drawings of simple wooden buildings which show us typical Japanese dwellings.

Still more exciting than what we can find out from the shell mounds and pit houses or from bronze objects discovered in grave mounds is what clay cylinders or *haniwa*, which surround mounds, show us. These were once filled with soil and set close together at the base of mounds to keep the heaped earth in place. Many different human societies have buried servants or women members of the royal family alive as sacrifices at the funeral of the lord and later have substituted images for the living people. But these cylinders were not found inside the mounds, but surrounding them outside. Some of them are plain, undecorated pottery tubes; others are surmounted by models of houses or other things. These *haniwa* provide us with miniature Japanese houses as well as with delightful people and animals. Even today *haniwa* are sometimes dug up.

The typical architecture of the early home which decorates the bronzes of the grave mounds and is on the clay cylinders is the pile house built of wood. Since this type of house is also common in the Philippine Islands, in Malaya, and in Indonesia, where floods and dampness are a problem, the people of these areas may all have learned it in a single place. Today, Japanese houses are still generally built so that they stand a little above the ground level.

Because chieftains claimed to have god ancestors, it is natural that their houses and early religious shrines were similar. Ruins of such a chieftain's house or of a shrine would tell us a good deal about these special buildings. But the Japanese built with wood rather than stone because wood was plentiful while hard rock was scarce. The wood most commonly used for building down through the ages has been *hinoki*, which is a very durable kind of cypress. In Japan most rock is a soft, porous, volcanic type.

The Ise Shrine at Ujiyamada, made up of the Inner and the Outer Shrines, is a wonderful example of buildings which were probably both a chieftain's palace and a sacred shrine. Even though the shrine is built of wood it is still authentic, because of the astonishing practice of tearing down an old structure and replacing it at regular intervals with a new one that follows the original design exactly. A new building is erected near the old one, which is not torn down until the one replacing it has been completed. The Ise Shrine was first erected in the seventh century A.D. and has been replaced every twenty years since then. Today's replica, the fifty-ninth, built in 1954, is almost exactly like the original buildings. Anthropologists call the people who brought this style of structure to Japan the Yayoi people, a name which comes from a street in the city of Tokyo where the first remnants of these ancestors of the Japanese were found. They are believed to have come from the South Sea Islands.

There are different ways of describing the Ise Shrine. Some claim that it is only glorified wooden huts, others, that it is in the very best Japanese artistic tradition because it is so simple, so elegantly undecorated. Part of its magic for the Japanese and of its charm for the foreign visitor is that it is the traditional shrine of the mythological sword and mirror of the divine Sun Goddess, Amaterasu. Every loyal Japanese hopes to make a pilgrimage to this holy spot, for it is the most sacred of Japanese shrines. Anyone who visits there will find people of every imaginable occupation walking along the pebbled paths through *torii* or sacred archways and beneath giant trees.

Even apart from its tradition, Ise is uniquely beautiful. It stands near a clear stream and is surrounded by mossy rocks and tremendous evergreens. Its absolute simplicity is startling. This is emphasized by the soft browns of unpainted cypress and the neutral shade and textured grace of the thatched roofs.

The Inner Shrine is the chief objective of pilgrims. It is a small, rectangular building, gabled at either end and standing on piles or piers which have been rammed into the earth. The walls are of heavy, bare wood. They are surrounded by a narrow gallery or porch with a railing. The building charms one because nothing about it is hidden or apologized for. Every pile, support, beam, post, and rafter is seen. The enormously thick thatch of the roof, which has been tied in bunches and lashed to the rafters, is so evenly shorn that it is the most beautiful part of the building. One can almost feel the grain and sheen of the wood; the roundness or squareness of the beams and rails; the order and trimness of the evenly laid roof. The shrine seems to be a part of nature itself.

The most important artistic value of truly Japanese buildings is the fact that they have been planned with the outdoors and the beauty of natural materials in mind. This closeness to nature is due not only to a sense of the beautiful but also to religious feeling. Hissing hot springs, roaring tidal waves, volcanoes, earthquakes, even a quiet sea, still mountains, gentle streams, and waving reeds are the homes of spirits or gods called *kami*. These gods accepted and lived in shrines especially built for them as ages passed.

From the earliest times *kami* have meant mystery; and when Buddhism and other religions reached Japan, the people soon saw that their naturalistic religion, based on *kami* and called *Shinto*, or the Way of the Gods, did not conflict with any new religion at all. The mystery of life was just as strong as ever. The Shinto gods were numerous, but the chief deity was still Amaterasu the Sun Goddess, from whom the imperial family descended.

One may wonder whether it is their belief that all nature, including many animals, is the home of spirit presences that has made the Japanese as patient as they are when natural disasters strike the islands. When earthquakes or tidal waves destroy great areas, they set to work to restore them. They look on themselves as only part of a physical world where accidents are expected from time to time.

An interesting mark of Shinto temples which ties them to nature is the use of arches or *torii*, just mentioned in connection with Ise. These arches often remind one of ceremonial gateways in China, India, or Korea. Whether they originated in some other country or whether they began, as some people think, as a perch for the sacred long-necked flying cocks which could have been the source of their name, *torii* are part of the Japanese landscape. They are most often made of beautiful logs or stone. Unfortunately, today they may be constructed of steel or concrete. Connected with ancient stones in formal gardens or palace grounds, they suggest mystery and religious feeling. It is ordinarily said that one takes the first step in purifying his soul when he walks through the arch of a *torii.*

The kinship between man and natural things so clearly displayed in Japanese architecture is described in an ancient Shinto liturgical song:

The Earth is the mother from whom all creatures have received their being and their life; and so all creatures join their voices in the universal hymn. The tall trees and the humble herbs, the stones, the sand, the earth we tread, the winds, the waves—all things, all, have a divine soul. The murmur of the breezes among the woods in springtime, the buzz of the insects among the moist autumn plants, are so many voices in the song of Earth. The sigh of the breeze, the roar of the torrent, are so many hymns of life in which all should rejoice. *

The Shinto point of view affects the feeling of Japanese not only toward natural objects, such as trees, mountains, and seas, but also toward the materials of which they are composed. Because trees hold beauty that only has to be released, beams and supports

---

* René Grosset, *The Civilizations of the East,* Alfred A. Knopf, Inc., New York, 1941, footnote, p. 15; taken from H. L. Joly, *Legend in Japanese Art,* Lane and Co., London and New York, 1908.

should be left exposed in building; often the very ir-regularity of a log adds to the pleasure of the viewer. The woods of Japan are treated so as to display all their natural beauty. Unpainted wood, often unvar-nished, shows its grain and suggests a mood. Modern decorators in the West call this emphasis on the qual-ity of materials and on usefulness in structure "func-tional." It has long been a part of Shinto tradition in Japan.

The attention paid to natural colors and textures of building materials is strongly emphasized in traditional homes and shrines. These are built of clay, tiles, wood, lacquer, textiles, straw, bamboo, and paper.

Clay is an ingredient of plaster which sometimes surfaces the outer walls of a house and often covers inner walls unless they are wooden. The color of plaster is artistically important. Sometimes plaster used on inside walls is tinted a smoky gray or creamy yellow; or, following an ancient fashion, it is variegated by mix-ing in crushed shells or iron fillings. Pure white plaster contrasts beautifully with the neutral shades of un-painted wood and straw matting or with the dark hues of serving tables, black cast-iron kettles, and brilliant lacquer bowls. It enhances the colors of decorations in the *tokonoma* or alcove, of which we shall speak later.

Tiles for the ridgepole of a thatch-roofed building,

or the whole roof of a Buddhist temple, are of pottery. It is hard to find anything in western architecture which gives one the feeling of a tiled roof. The commonest kind is gray-blue, laid curve to curve, in long ridges, upright and inverted, sloping down from ridgepole to eaves in sinuous, almost living lines.

But the basic material of Japanese building is clearly wood. In a castle for a noble or a home for an ordinary family this is so. *Hinoki*, a Japanese cypress, is plentiful, and stays in good condition for as long as twelve or thirteen centuries if it is well cared for.

Using wood construction makes a home or a great hall more adaptable than one with internal walls of plaster, brick, or stone. Wooden walls can be movable partitions or can be lattices called *shoji*, which are covered with translucent paper. Partitions which slide along grooves set into the floor and the crossbeams of the ceiling are called *fusuma*. They can be pulled out or pushed back to make a room larger or smaller. Sliding walls like these change the feeling of a place, too, because they can open a view into other areas or close in a room snugly.

Sometimes the space between the overhead beam and the ceiling is filled in with bamboo latticing or with wood decorated with carving or pierced designs. In some famous buildings these *ramma* are exquisite.

Ordinarily windows are papered lattices protected from the weather or at night by a narrow porch which is closed with wooden shutters. Ceilings are often made of thin, slightly overlapping panels of unpainted wood a foot or so wide. These are held in place by crossing parallel strips which are invisibly nailed in place. In fine buildings these panels may be cut from one large tree and carefully planed to keep the natural design and continuity of the grain.

This emphasis on the quality of wood is carried even further in furniture. Furniture is so noticeably absent in most Japanese houses that this may seem to be a strange statement; but this absence really emphasizes the character of the furniture that is there. No chairs or tables stand about. Even a chest of drawers is usually low enough to be pushed away into a built-in cupboard or closet, or at least to be hidden by a screen. People sit with their feet beneath them or on cushions which are stowed away when they are not being used. Meals are served on low tables which are taken out of sight when the meal is over. Beds are quilts or *futon* which are spread on matting floor sections or *tatami*, and then are folded up during the day and closeted. Cupboards in the kitchen take care of utensils, and only built-in drawers may indicate that some part of the house is a kitchen.

The size of an ordinary house is traditionally based on the *tatami* unit. The name of the floor section comes from a Japanese word which means to roll up, for probably these mats used to be rolled up and put away after sleeping. Gradually they became permanent sections of the floor which were padded and covered with matting.

The effect of rooms dominated by wood, plaster, paper, and matting is one of harmony. Space, airiness, and restfulness are suggested at every turn. When everything is thrown open, the garden, however small, is the focus; making use of natural colors and simple lines, it relates the house to outdoors. Even the most rustic fisherman's hut, a little farmhouse, or an ordinary town house seems to show that its master or mistress never forgets what is beyond the room. A rock, a bent tree standing near the entrance, a blossoming fruit tree, or a clump of small bamboo often link the indoors to the garden. If there is no space for even a tiny garden, perhaps a *torii* guarded by an embracing tree or an ancient, twisted wisteria forms part of the entryway.

Shinto influence is still strong in the traditional Japanese home. Space and emptiness suggest the influence. Avoiding what has no real use in a room makes everything that is there important because it is necessary. Highlighting colors by placing them next to monotones gives pleasure. A red lacquer box may stand on a low ebony table against a screen of natural-colored paper. Glistening white bean curds in a black bowl may be placed on a serving table near a basin of shining green vegetables. A brilliant *kimono* may contrast as if by accident with the straw *tatami* as the wife serves the family. The colors of a scroll hanging above a vase of flowers in the *tokonoma* or alcove or of beautiful stones or shells arranged on a low table beneath a favorite hanging are all made more delightful because of the contrast between soft tones and vivid ones.

This love of natural beauty dignifies everyday life; and this dignity in even small things is characteristic of the Japanese. They know that the most ordinary act can be significant if it is performed in an artistic way.

When Buddhism was introduced into Japan in the sixth century, it had a definite influence on the Japanese home and shrines. This influence was not at all like that of Shinto, yet that part of it which is most commonly seen in Japanese houses has been adapted to Shinto use.

The *tokonoma* or alcove, where beautiful or religious objects are displayed, has become an important part of the Japanese home, though it seems to be of

Buddhist origin. There are several explanations of the way the *tokonoma* came to have its place. One is that the *tokonoma* was once a raised platform where a bed could be spread so that it would not come into contact with the damp earth floor. But this simple theory is not widely held, for although no buildings remain of the time when the alcove was introduced to Japanese life, many picture scrolls show us how it came about. Scroll artists of the Heian and Kamakura periods sometimes made a practice of removing the roofs of houses they painted so that one can easily see details of the interiors.

The *tokonoma* seems to have grown from the *shoin* bay, which was first used as a small study alcove, opening from a larger hall and lighted by its own window. Sometimes this little bay extended from the house wall and was sheltered by a separate roof, much like the bay window of modern western homes. The *shoin* bay at first provided a place where a Buddhist priest could study or read. Later it was a library alcove with book shelves and still with the overhanging roof which seemed to shelter it from the larger room from which it opened, even when it had no outside window of its own. In Zen Buddhist architecture this shelf space was used for memorial tablets.

All these stages make it clear that the *tokonoma*

has a religious origin as the priest's study, then as a place to keep memorial scrolls. It gradually became the place for Buddhist images or offerings of flowers in the temple or the home. From these stages it became and still is the decorative focus of the home, but it has a deeper meaning than decoration. The arrangement of whatever is placed there suggests serious meditation or even worship. A time came in Buddhist history when Zen Buddhists no longer wanted to use images of Buddha or his followers. Their substitution of flowers or something else of simple beauty aided the development of the *tokonoma* as a center of what is beautiful and full of meaning.

Objects that recall family experiences, like a sword, a pair of military boots, a pilgrim's staff, a colored stone from some mountain top or sacred stream, or a beautiful vase or bowl may help the members of the family to relive times of danger, pleasure, poignancy, or worship and thankfulness.

Buddhism changed the architecture of religious buildings more than that of homes. There could scarcely be a greater contrast than that between the Ise Shrine and Horyuji, the oldest Buddhist temple in Japan, near Nara. While Ise is starkly and yet softly simple, Horyuji is a place of thirty-three buildings, a pagoda, and tiers of roofs under which several hundred national treasures are housed. Like Ise, Horyuji is built of wood. It is thought to be the oldest existing temple in Japan and perhaps the oldest wooden structure in the world. It was founded in 607 by Prince Shotoku, the beloved regent who made Buddhism respectable by becoming a Buddhist himself. Horyuji is situated in open countryside, and its tree-lined avenues leading to the Chinese curved roofs, which rise one above another toward the sky, give the visitor a feeling of pleasant peacefulness. Although it has so many buildings, it seems to belong to the landscape where it stands. The pine trees which rise here and there in the courts or lean against the colonnades or peep into the temple grounds from outside only soften it and enhance it. The pines play a special part because of their deep green color.

While both Ise and Horyuji are built of wood, Ise is the soft, neutral color of aged wood itself. Horyuji, on the other hand, was once painted red; now that red has faded to an indescribable shade which contrasts with white stuccoed walls, blue-green lattices on the windows, and tiles of gray. This red suits the Chinese-inspired temple with its up-tilted eaves, its pagoda, and its decorative gateways and pillars. Horyuji is rich but not ornate. Its plan is unified and well constructed so that its most famous buildings, the Great South

Gate, the Kondo or Main Hall, the Five-Storied Pagoda, the Temple of the Middle Palace, the delightful cloister for nuns, and others, all belong together as in a planned motif.

Horyuji seems to express the first great impression of early Buddhism on the relatively uncultured people of the Japanese islands. Gilt, color, and decoration are all used in these religious buildings, but they are intended to express the richness of the teaching that Buddhist visitors were bringing from the mainland.

Common Clay to Priceless Porcelain

People of ancient times created some of the world's earliest and most beautiful art from clay. Intending at first just to make containers for water or grain, they were soon unable to resist an urge to vary shapes in more and more pleasing ways. When a pebble or a stick marred the clay's smoothness, this accident may have suggested incised decorations, knobs, or ridges which proved to be delightful innovations.

People who lived in Japan between two and three thousand years before the Christian era shaped their dark gray earthenware, or pottery, by hand. The potter's wheel had not yet reached them from China. They baked what they made in the sun or at low heat and decorated it in two particular ways. One was to mark it with a design made by pressing rope, or perhaps something like rope wrapped around a stick, into the surface of the finished jar while the clay was still moist. Another was to scar the clay piece with a sharp stick in a crisscross fashion, making what are called mat designs. The name given to this early pottery with wavy rope or crisscross mat markings is Jomon ware. Anthropologists call the people who made it the Jomon people.

This early, dark gray earthenware suggests that its makers were experimenting with clay, for what they made is free and varied. Not even the whirling of a wheel controlled its form by centrifugal laws. Hands alone shaped it for use.

Clay figurines or *dogu* also belong to this period of Japanese history. They are Japan's earliest sculpture. These figurines have been found in burial places and on the sites of homes. Some of them are very small and may have been hung around the neck as charms. Larger ones were made to stand. These were probably idols. Often they have strange faces and staring eyes that suggest magical powers. Some of these pieces have a curiously modern, almost surrealistic quality. Anthropologists claim that no other neolithic culture has produced idols that compare with these. Decoration of their vessels and their idols suggest that the Jomon people probably had some connection with the mainland and the Ainu people.

The Korean peninsula had been strongly influenced by Chinese who had fled there to escape unsettled times at home as early as the third century B.C. when the Han dynasty was beginning. Japanese people of the age after the Jomon were almost certainly actual immigrants from Korea, as well as people from the South Seas. These new people of the islands are called Yayoi, named as we already know for the place in Tokyo where remnants of their culture were dug up.

While the Jomon people made dark gray pottery, the Yayoi sometimes produced a deep red pottery as well. They turned their pieces on wheels and baked them at high temperatures. Shapes were symmetrical and plain, and designs were incised geometrical patterns. Even though this pottery is more expertly made than Jomon ware, it does not have the life or boldness of the earlier age. It seems as though the potters were holding their feelings back or following rules of some kind. They made vessels that were well shaped and precisely decorated but which said less than the hand molded ones of the less civilized Jomon people. Both peoples lived in the islands during the period of gradual change from the earlier to the later group, but they do not seem to have had much contact with each other. The holding back or restraint which became characteristic of Japanese art began with the Yayoi people.

The Yayoi grave mounds that yielded the potteries we have been talking about also yielded *haniwa*, the clay cylinders filled with earth and set at the base of mounds from which we learned something about house designs. The *haniwa* were decorated with figurines, too, and these delightful figures of people and animals are not at all like the mysterious, staring idols of the Jomon people. While the sculptured figures of this period are still stiff, partly because they are mounted on the body of a cylinder, they are beautifully shaped in the round and full of life.

Some of the *haniwa* are small; some as much as two or three feet high. They combine the feeling of children's work with a sophisticated touch and have as little self-consciousness as toys. People in court dress, men in armor, dancers poised in action, musicians, falconers, or women carrying children are to be found among them. Sometimes the men have their hair arranged like the pony tails girls wear in the western countries today, but after an ancient Chinese fashion. Horses are lively and dashing. Birds, boats, and houses join the other designs that are found.

Clay appears again and again in the story of Japan's arts and crafts because cultural progress is often recorded in the transition from clay pottery to porcelain. Every conquest, every invasion by outsiders is likely to leave its mark on a nation's ceramics. This has been true in Japan; and yet, even through a succession of such fresh influences, the Japanese touch is strong.

New contacts were of several kinds, and they came from a number of sources. The first new contact came from the mainland about the fifth century A.D. Vessels that had for a long time been used in Confucian ceremonies in China now reached Japan by way of Silla, the southeastern part of Korea, and started the making of a new kind of pottery. This is called Iwabe or Sue' ware. It is important because it was a technical advance over the earlier earthernware potteries.

Iwabe or Sue' ware vessels were dark gray in color. They were usually bulbous in shape and stood on hol-

low stems which had rectangular or triangular per-
forations. They had large mouths, and often extra
spouts. Sometimes small human or animal figures
peeped out from the shoulders of the vessels. This way
of making pottery became popular and was used for
centuries. As time passed it was sometimes partly
covered with green glaze, the first use of glaze in
Japanese ceramics.

Glaze became curiously important in the story of
ceramics. It was often taken as a sign of progress—as
if civilizations, like children, enjoy something that
glistens and feels smooth to the touch. The Egyptians
are famous for their beautiful glazes. These are so
beautiful that one almost forgets about the designs
which may not equal those of some other peoples. In
the case of the Greeks, form and design are so lovely
that glaze becomes secondary. But the Chinese, the
Koreans, and the Japanese believed that glaze was a
highly important criterion of their workmanship.
Underglaze, painting in enamels, and overglaze were
perfected. Some of the examples have become priceless museum pieces all over the world.

The second new influence on Japanese ceramics
was Buddhism. This reached Japan in 552 A.D. when
the king of Kudara, Korea, presented Buddhist scriptures to the Japanese imperial court. This began

Japan's Buddhist age. When the new capital was built at Nara during the seventh century, it was patterned after the Chinese T'ang dynasty one. Chinese Buddhist influences dominated the arts.

Glazing pottery with more than one color was now learned from the mainland. The pottery had a rather rough surface; but green, yellow, and white glazes applied separately or combined, produced dramatic effects. The Shosoin collection in Nara today includes some pieces of this work which are thought to date back to the eighth century.

In the ninth century a glazing method called *celadon* came to Japan from China. The origin of the name is still being debated but it clearly refers to a special green, blue, or blue-green color. Celadon may have begun in China in an attempt to produce jade color on ceramics by using iron in the glaze, for the color of jade was greatly admired. Celadon later came to include many shades and even a variety of whites. Such glazing had to be done in high-fired kilns. The best Japanese ones were in Owari province where Sue' wares continued to be made. By the twelfth century a village called Seto, which is near the Owari kilns, became the center for pottery, or *setomono*. What is known as Seto ware came from Temmoku ware, which was also of Chinese origin. The name grew from the T'ien Mu hills in Chekiang province where tea bowls of black ware were used by priests in the Zen Buddhist monasteries. Although the bowls were not made there but in still another location, the name of the hills gave rise to the Japanese Temmoku. Seto ware is dark brown or black, with a thick glaze of purplish black shot with lines or flecks of light brown.

During the Kamakura period (1185–1338) when Kyoto was still the cultural center and Kamakura the hub of the military dictators, militarism was glorified. This was the Japanese age of knights, the *samurai*, and of *Bushido*, the Way of the Sword. Zen Buddhism, which had developed in the eighth century A.D., now suddenly became popular. This form of the religion stresses a simple, personal religious life without scriptures, ceremony, or creed. It appealed to active military men who had grown disgusted with the complicated religious rituals and overly refined court life of Kyoto. To them Zen was like a fresh breeze.

The potter's sense of form and color seemed to be sharpened in this rare atmosphere. He went to his work with a new vision of freedom and adventure. In 1223 A.D. a Japanese priest named Doyen is said to have taken Kato Shirazaemon, a Japanese potter, with him to study the work of the Sung dynasty potters who were famous for their fine ceramics. When the potter returned he set up his own kiln in Seto and made a thin purplish-black ware, glazed in brown with an uneven over-glaze of black.

During this Kamakura period a small apparently incidental affair became influential in Japanese life and arts, especially in ceramics. This was ritual tea drinking. It had begun with Zen Buddhists, first in China and then in Japan, who drank tea to keep themselves awake at their long studies and meditations. Tea was not grown in Japan until the ninth century.

But by the time of the military dictators in Kamakura drinking tea from beautiful handle-less cups or bowls was not only a fashion, but a cult. In the fifteenth century Shonzui, a master potter, went to China's famous Ching-te Chen porcelain works to study their methods. Back in Japan he had to use imported clay since none suitable for porcelain had yet been discovered there.

Strong Korean influence affected Japanese potters a second time during the Momoyama period (1568–1615). Hideyoshi, one of the three great dictators of this time, liked to do everything on a grand scale. He held tea parties of such size as had never been heard of. On one celebrated occasion he invited everyone to the Kitano Tea Party. Rich and poor were all in-

cluded; but the poor had to bring their own hot water kettles, their own cups, and their mats to sit on. Another party was so lavish that an ancient temple, Sambo-in, was restored and enlarged for the occasion.

The effect of all this on the ceramic arts was enormous. Wealthy people began to compete in having the finest of everything connected with the ceremony of drinking tea. Potters worked under pressure to improve their products and to create imaginative designs. Master potters soared to fame. Korean styles were in particular demand.

One of the most famous kinds of tea bowls was made by a Korean family. It was called *Raku* ware. The name came from a gold seal meaning contentment which Hideyoshi gave a member of the family. This ware has been made in Kyoto, the traditional center of the tea ceremony, for centuries, and descendants of the original family, which has come to be called by the name Raku, still produce it. It is made of coarse clay shaped by hand. After it is lightly fired, it is gray or brown. First it was black glazed, then red, green, yellow, or white were used. It is usually not decorated but sometimes it has a light design in contrasting glaze. Since the bowls are thick and do not let the heat through easily, they are particularly prized for tea drinking.

Raku ware has such a long history that its individual styles have come to have names, sometimes taken from those of potters. Koetsu, who was also famous for his painting, lacquer work, and calligraphy, is well known for his Mount Fuji Raku ware. Potters of the illustrious family itself could not match his work.

Near the end of the sixteenth century, a prince of Satsuma, in Osumi province, brought seventeen Korean potters to Japan. They set up their kilns and their wares were called Satsuma after the prince. It was glazed earthernware which was almost as fine as porcelain, and particularly liked for its crackled surface. In addition to the plain crackled glaze, Satsuma ware was decorated with colored brocade designs, and with such motifs as dragons or phoenixes. White Satsuma, which is undecorated but covered with finely cracked ivory glaze, became especially famous. As time passed Satsuma ware was considered one of the finest of Japanese ceramics. It is still made but imitations of old designs are often disappointing.

A favorite kind of Korean pottery was Shino, which was made at Seto. It is thick and coarse, irregularly shaped, and covered by a heavy bubbly white glaze applied unevenly, and sometimes decorated with abstract designs of reddish iron oxide. It gets its name from the tea-master Shino Shoshin who lived in the fifteenth century, but it was being made well into the nineteenth century.

Korean influence is probably most clearly recognizable in pottery made at the port, Karatsu, which has long been actively connected with Korean trade. Korean potters came here when they were brought in by Hideyoshi to teach Japanese craftsmen their skills. It was also here that kilns patterned after those of Korea were introduced to Japan during the same period. There are several varieties of Karatsu ware but they can be identified by their characteristic blue-black base covered with a cast-iron glaze which is then smeared with gray, brown, or white glaze. Sometimes a design is lightly brushed on like a suggestion. Students of ceramics flock to Karatsu and sometimes make delightful finds of old Karatsu ware fragments when they dig among the ruined kilns in the surrounding hills.

While pottery was made in Japan by both Koreans and Japanese, and while porcelain was beginning to reach Japan by way of Korea, a great search for fine porcelain clay had been going on in Japan. Meantime such clay was being imported from the mainland. Shonzui, who had gone to China in the fifteenth century to study porcelain making, had as we know to work with imported clay.

Fine porcelains from China spurred the search more and more, for by now the imported pieces were almost transparent, and they rang like a bell at the touch of a finger. These could only be made from a fine-grained clay, one producing a substance like the pearly coating of shells. The word *porcelain* originates with shells.

At last a Korean potter discovered the longed-for clay in the Arita district of Hizen. Potters flocked to the source and set to work. The wares they made were exported from the port Imari by the Dutch traders who soon flooded Europe with famous "old Imari" which took its name from the town. This first Imari ware was strongly shadowed by a Korean touch. It usually had a white base covered with translucent glaze and was decorated with blue designs such as landscapes or children at play. Later, the Chinese way of using colored overglazes was practiced. Brocade designs covered some pieces. Again scenes illustrating historical events were favored. Some amusing items portray sailing ships bringing in Dutch traders who can be identified by their large red noses.

When Japan closed her doors to the world early in the seventeenth century, her own arts flourished more than ever. In the middle of the seventeenth century new varieties of Imari ware were developed in Arita. One of them was Kakiemon, named for the man who made it. Kakiemon ware's clear white, enamelled in soft orange red, grass green, or lilac blue, and sometimes touched with yellow or turquoise, frequently based on underglazed blue, became world-famous. It suggests the great K'ang Hsi porcelains of China, but it had its own character. Kakiemon's taste in design was strongly Japanese. A few flowers, a blossoming tree, bamboos and a tiger, children—these were typical.

Even though foreign trade was now forbidden in Japan, some of the Kakiemon ware reached Europe through the few Dutch traders who were allowed to stay on at Deshima. The ware became enormously popular and was copied in Delft, Holland, in Meissen, Germany, and in Worcester, England.

Probably the most technically perfect porcelain ever made in Japan is Nabeshima, which takes its name from the house of the lord for whom it was especially created. It has abstract purely decorative designs, usually outlined in blue. The result is regular and pleasing. Many people think that Nabeshima ware is more truly Japanese in its feeling than Kakiemon.

During the seventeenth and eighteenth centuries many porcelain workers were busy producing pieces considered the greatest art of the period. A golden age of the potters' skill had arrived. The early, handshaped clay utensils of the prehistoric shell mounds and of the grave mounds had advanced with the help of examples from China to being one of the most celebrated arts of the Japanese.

Two master potters must be singled out. They are

Ninsei (1598–1666) and Kenzan (1663–1743). Ninsei used gold freely as a glaze and also as a dust sprinkled on. His designs were usually pictorial and sometimes seemed gaudy to the western eye. Kenzan had a free, abstract touch. He liked to use simple, native subjects in his designs.

When Japan began world trade again with the Restoration in 1867, porcelain was a major export item. The Japanese kept on making their fine old patterns but also experimented with new styles in the hope of satisfying the demand for cheaper goods and modern tastes. As the years passed, hundreds of western potters went to Japan to study under her masters whose works are to be seen in great international exhibitions all over the world. Japanese methods were copied commercially but few could compete with them.

Today many people have become deeply interested in the revival of Japanese folk arts. This is especially true of ceramics. Dr. Yanagi Soetsu has had an important part in creating interest in Japanese folk arts both in Japan and abroad. He founded the Japanese Folk Art Society with the help of Shoji Hamada and others, in 1931. This society established a folk art museum in Tokyo in 1938 and then in two other locations. These have led to the opening of folk craft shops in many places.

Not only have ancient crafts been preserved through the leadership of men like Dr. Yanagi and Shoji Hamada, they are again being created. The famous English potter, Bernard Leach, joined the Japanese Folk Art Society early in its history. He has greatly influenced western potting during the last twenty years because of his work with Japanese folk art masters. Shoji Hamada studied under Leach in England for four years and so the two men have joined their efforts.

Today Shoji Hamada is thought of as closest to a true folk artist in Japan. He lives simply, will not sign his works, and creates pieces which show the touch of ancient Korea or of early English, or follows the traditions of his own country's folk potteries. He has also developed two remarkable new techniques. These are drip painting and salt glaze which seem only further to emphasize his love of pure, sturdy form and deep dull blues, grays, and browns which have become so well loved all over the world.

Japanese folk pottery is usually extremely simple in both shape and decoration. It emphasizes heavy, subdued colors and running glazes that appear to be almost accidentally attractive.

One could easily list a half dozen special types—

Ouda teapots which are covered with blue-green glaze; lidded pickle jars of pleasing shapes; everyday cooking pots with side handles, and knob lids, which are notable because of their reddish clay partly covered with running green glaze—yet these would be no more than a small sampling of beautiful utilitarian items in many a market place.

When all these pieces in the story of clay and porcelain have been brought together, the resulting picture still may not describe the beauty of an ordinary flower vase. Here is one in front of me. It was made in modern Japan. It did not cost much, and yet it enhances every spray of flowers or foliage put in it. It is rather tall, narrowed only slightly at the high-shouldered mouth. It is shaped of coarse-grained clay, which gives a rough finish. Though certainly turned on a wheel, it seems to have been quickly touched with some broad blade. Blade marks suggest thickness and heaviness like the grain and feel of wet cement. The color is pale gray, and against this background a few dark brush marks suggest bamboo twigs and a few disconnected leaves. That is the beauty of this vase: that it only suggests shape, texture, design, and color. Whatever it holds becomes the only definiteness. The vase is, as it should be, simply a container for flowers.

Shining Swords to Cast-iron Kettles

It is easiest to think of Japanese metalwares as belonging to two main groups. The first is armor and swords; the second iron utensils for everyday use and for ceremonial tea drinking. In addition there are many special art objects such as the beautiful metal lanterns of Nara.

Ancient swords and armor found in grave mounds

tell us that the Japanese knew how to work iron as long ago as the second century A.D. Yet the metal was so scarce in early times that iron tools sometimes stood for money. Debts to feudal lords could be paid in iron spades or pounds of iron.

Iron was cherished for its connection with mythology as well as for its scarcity. The very islands, the story of beginnings says, were created from drops of water falling from Izanami's sword when he lifted it out of the sea. The Sun Goddess, Amaterasu, followed him in the family of gods. A sword, curved metal jewels, and a metal mirror are the sacred emblems of her shrines. These three things also became emblems of the emperor, who according to legend was a descendant of the Sun Goddess. For centuries no one but the ruling family dreamed of owning a sword, and even the emperor's swords were kept in Shinto shrines. By the eighth century nobles made a show of wearing swords, although they were only wooden dummies indicating the wearer's rank.

Real swords, beautifully made, were considered the most significant gifts for formal occasions. When emissaries went to China, they presented splendid swords to the high officers of the Chinese court. One cannot help wondering what the Chinese thought about this, as swords did not have the same traditional importance for them. But since at that time in history they considered the "dwarfs of the Eastern Ocean" rather barbarous, perhaps the gift of a sword seemed natural. Certainly they had to admire its workmanship.

In the thirteenth century, when military dictators were the real authority in Japan, they took pride in their own swords. Only one sword was permitted to a family, and it was in the care of the most respected member of that family.

Some of the early Minamoto generals of this period encouraged iron mining on their lands and patronized smiths, encouraging them to improve their art. Later the Minamoto clan claimed two unusually fine glades as their own. Many traditions grew up around them in the years that followed. One story was that the smith had succeeded so well in refining the iron to steel and then in tempering the steel because he had fasted and prayed.

Philosophy and craftsmanship were combined in swordmaking to an astonishing degree. The story of the Minamoto swordmaker grew with passing time. Smiths who were about to make swords after the traditional patterns purified themselves by ritual ceremonies, put on white robes, and used charms to keep off wicked spirits. To make a noble blade, the craftsman must be noble.

Thus swordmaking became a real art. While Kamakura was the center of the military dictatorship, even the Chinese wanted to buy swords from Japan. They became one of the most important items of trade between the two countries.

Making a sword was a difficult and painstaking job. Thin metal strips had to be forged together, cut, laid on each other, and then forged again. Tempering, polishing, and final shaping took weeks, without allowing for the days spent on the magnificent decorations created by inlaying other metals on both hilt and guard. Such beautiful swords were made in Japan that they came to belong peculiarly to that country. No swords can match the symbolic ones of the Japanese craftsman.

There was a quality about these swords that went beyond their perfection. A man who carried a certain sword had the responsibility of living up to its reputation. Some swords were known as preservers of peace; some, as inspirers of daring. The special attribute of a sword must be thought of before it was drawn from its sheath; for once the sword was bared, it had to be used before it could be thrust back.

Armor was also extremely important in the lives of the military men. Japanese helmets and armor are among the most picturesque in the world. When a *samurai* was in full battle dress, he was truly resplendent. Armor was handed down from one generation to another as an ancestral treasure, so that donning it had particular significance. Ancient descriptions mention gorgeous silk robes over which the body armor, probably first of leather and later of lacquer, was laced with Chinese leather. Decorations tended to disappear. Trappings of bright colors and gilded saddles, as well as eagle-feathered arrows and rattan bows, were gradually replaced by steel daggers and swords. Practical metal helmets and armor were more serviceable than gold lacquer. Special armor made of metal parts and called "grand armor" provided real protection. Yet sword guards became a specialized art, for they were so beautifully decorated that they have become museum pieces.

During the centuries when arms making was being honored in military circles, iron was also used for everyday things. Axheads and blades of many varieties; teakettles and teakettle stands; tongs; locks; scissors; and the peculiarly human short-handled rakes were all commonly made of iron. These iron tools and utensils are all inviting; they look as if they were made to use, and yet they have been designed with a natural sense of beauty.

Iron hot-water kettles have an unusual degree of

this inviting quality, for kettles always seem to have a kind of personality. Those made in Morioka, for example, suggest a dumpy comfort because of their shape. Even the handle curves in a sympathetic arc above the wide, round lid with its ball knob. The only decorations are alternating rows of small, beadlike bumps that cover the upper half of the body. Other kettles from the same area are conical in shape with the top cut off for the lid space. They have large decorative knobs and elaborate handles suspend them over the fire. They are beautiful in a dignified way. Kettles from Ashiya have ceremonial simplicity.

Everyday kettles, whether round and comfortable or hump-shouldered or squat, whether with spouts that seem to have grown from the body or stick out oddly or suggest disdain for the world, all imply singing sounds and warmth. Handles play their part, too, for they may be fixed and straight or hinged so that they fall to one side, or take postures which give quite a rakish air to an otherwise humdrum kettle.

The short-handled rakes that the Japanese housewife habitually uses to stir the coal of her brazier have an appeal akin to that of the kettles. One instinctively reaches out to take one in his hand because it looks so useful and welcoming. Their only decoration is usually an incised or perforated pattern.

The charm underlying all cast iron and wrought iron things comes from both texture and color. One remembers the molding process of the first and the heating and hammering necessary for the second and feels the grain and texture of the metal. But even more, the blue-black hues of dull, unpolished iron or the mellow sheen of pieces worn smooth by use delights us. One is aware that they are cold when not in use and lastingly warm when they have been near the fire. Their texture and color make every brilliant shade which comes near them the more beautiful by contrast. So in a Japanese room they enhance lacquer, wood, straw, and all the shades of pottery and porcelain.

Treasures from a Tree

When we hear the word *lacquer*, we probably think of different kinds of things. Lacquer has been used in many ways since its story began more than three thousand years ago in China. We may visualize lacquered tables, stands, chairs, boxes, and trays and see butterflies or phoenixes, or bamboo and ancient figures in the decorations. Such pieces as these use lacquer as a paint. We may also think of rice bowls or teacups or vases which seem extremely fragile because they bend in our fingers. Because these are made on a fiber rather than a wood base, they are very supple. One may remember magnificent museum treasures, too.

But when I hear the word, I think of a small lacquered god or idol I once had. It had a small door in its back where one could tuck a prayer written on a slip of paper. Its hollowed-out wooden core had been coated with clay, molded to make the face, ears, headdress, and the loosely lying arms and upturned palms which rested in the folds of its Buddhist gown. The clay was painted with many coats of lacquer, which had formed a kind of smooth, glossy shell. But the surface was a soft, faded red. Touches of blue, green, and gold edged the folds and ridges.

In its natural state lacquer is unappealing. It is the sap of the varnish tree, *Rhus verniciflua*, a sumac native to China.

Some of the emissaries who went from Japan to China saw beautiful lacquer work there and wanted to find out how to produce it in their own country. For a long time the only way seemed to be to import the raw sap from the mainland, because none of the trees grew in the islands. But after experimenting for a time, the Japanese successfully cultivated lacquer trees.

Preparing lacquer is a most tedious process. The sap must be drawn from trees at least ten years old; it must be heated slowly to evaporate much of the liquid; then it must be strained to remove all impurities. Objects to be lacquered should be perfectly smooth. Every tiny crack is carefully filled with putty and then sanded down. Coat after coat of lacquer varnish is put on, and this step must be taken in moist air. Each coat has to be dried slowly and then sanded down before the next one is applied. Even the smallest rough place would make a blemish in the final coat.

Bowls and canisters or other containers, which are sometimes made over a cloth or fiber base, assume their final shape only because many coatings of lacquer gradually give them body. It may take up to thirty applications to complete such a piece, and each one has to be dried and made perfectly smooth. You can imagine how much time is needed for such a process.

Lacquer workers became expert very slowly. Perfection was reached in several stages. At first lacquer was thought of as just a durable paint. While the capital was at Nara, it was used in everyday ways; for painting boxes, trays, musical instruments, rice bowls, ladles, and vases. It could be applied to many different surfaces, such as clay, wood, bamboo, cloth, and leather. At a time when porcelain was still too rare and expensive except for special purposes, lacquered food bowls, rice buckets, water buckets, and wine cups were in common use. The lacquer paint coated these objects with a durable surface that did not leak and withstood heat. These utensils were usually brilliant red or ebony.

Colors were produced in lacquer by a number of discoveries. Cinnabar added to the lac made red; gamboge made yellow; pig's gall and vegetable oil made amber; but red was always the most beautiful.

Color made the utensils beautiful, but they had another delightful quality. Wooden water buckets, rice containers, or any large pieces showed their construction. The framework was not covered over at all. Wooden staves bound together by a bamboo hoop like a barrel were not hidden. Looking at such utensils, many of which are still being made, one thinks of the simplicity of the Ise Shrine and of how functional much Japanese art is.

As time passed a good many different ways of decorating lacquer came into style. Gold and silver decorations were especially popular during the Nara period. These were put on in the form of gold and silver leaf, often in geometric designs; or by dusting gold or silver powder over a stencil to make a pattern. Sometimes decorations were painted on lacquer in oils. Again, mother-of-pearl was pressed into a soft clay base which was then sanded down so that it showed when a last clear lacquer varnish was put on. Flowers, birds, trees, and mythological creatures like phoenixes and dragons were favorites. Fruit and paulownia leaves were also popular. Some patterns came to be almost standard, but sometimes surprise designs showed up— a staring-eyed red crab on a jet black background or a jade green cicada or praying mantis hanging on a bending blade of grass against a golden base.

Much of the beautiful lacquer work, even that thought of as fine art, was made by anonymous craftsmen rather than artists. For a long time it was not considered a treasure nor put into collections or museums. But even if lacquer making began as a craft rather than an art, it has long been a way of expressing artistic feeling. An elegant court scene on a screen or a design made of no more than unattached wooden wheels swirling in a current of water on the lid of a lacquer cosmetic box are both enchanting, though different. This cosmetic box, preserved from the Kyoto period, is greatly prized. One glance at even a photograph makes it easy to understand why. The curving lines of the swirling current and the motion of the half-submerged wheels at their various angles describe an everyday incident, but one ruled by universal laws. It is in the Shinto tradition. The work is done in the gold dust method and highlighted by inserts of mother-of-pearl. When one lifts the lid he discovers, contrasting with the bold simplicity of the outside, a gentle pattern made up of butterflies, birds, and chrysanthemums.

Another kind of lacquer was monochrome black or red painted on a carved wooden base, coat after coat, until the piece seemed to be made of solid lacquer. It had an opaque quality and a texture suggestive of soapstone or amber. This technique came from China during the time of the military dictatorships and appealed enormously to the *shoguns*.

In the fourteenth and fifteenth centuries, a time came when Japan could teach China something about the arts. The Japanese were making such beautiful lacquer that the Chinese came to find out how they did it. The visitors particularly wanted to know how gold sprinkling and raised relief were perfected.

Lacquer had become one of the fine arts in Japan. There were famous lacquer artists like Koami Michinaga and Igarashi Shinsai. Often, too, great painters provided designs for lacquer artists, and so the two arts were combined. By the seventeenth century when trade between Asia and Europe was flourishing, the Japanese were so expert in lacquer that their work entranced the traders who saw it. When they went home, they tried to imitate it. The process they developed was called "japanning." Cabinetmakers in England experimented with an asphaltum base varnish, covering it with clear copal and baking it on. They could not come near to matching imported lacquer. Real lacquer could not be produced in Europe because the lac trees did not grow there. Especially hard varnishes, still called "japans" today, are often used to cover parts of motor cars or clock dials.

Images of Gods and Men

The little idol mentioned in the last chapter was an illustration of both lacquer and sculpture, although we usually think of stone when we talk about sculpture. Because Japan is a land where not even moderately good stone, much less fine marble, is found, her sculptors have used clay, bronze, wood, and lacquer or some combination of these materials. Perhaps we may miss the unique beauty of finely chiseled work; yet Japanese sculpture is beautiful and important.

The story of this sculpture could begin with the crude, symbolic staring gods and amulets that the shell mound people made, but *haniwa*, the lively little clay figurines of the grave mounds, were the first to represent realistic human beings and animals, showing their feelings and personalities. Some *haniwa* were exhibited in the National Gallery of Art in Washington, D.C., in the winter of 1960. They were set in a field of pebbles softened only by sparse plantings of bamboo. Although these figures were made so long ago by artisans rather than by artists or sculptors, they were so alive and so modern in feeling that people who saw them often smiled in delight.

Tori Bushi was the first great Japanese sculptor. He was a saddler at a time when a horse's trappings were decorated with incised bronze pieces. Since he was the grandson of a Buddhist immigrant, it does not surprise us that his famous work, the bronze Tori Bushi Trinity at Horyuji (623 A.D.), shows Buddhist influence. Buddhist art of this time, the seventh century, included the magnificent wall carvings or reliefs at Tung-Huang and Lung Men along the Silk Road, northwest of China. Although this way of carving was already old-fashioned in China, it influenced the

Tori Bushi Trinity. The figures of this work barely come forward from the background, and the background itself has only slightly raised decorations.

Another bronze, the Yakushi Trinity at Yakushiji near Nara, shows outside influence also. These three large figures include the seated Buddha, God of the Eastern Paradise, flanked by two standing ones, Gakko and Nikko, who are gods of the sun and the moon. These were made about 696 or even later. They show life and grandeur which makes us think of the T'ang dynasty in China of the same time, or even of the Aryan influence of India, which was of course the home of Buddhism. Some authorities feel that this group is affected by the stone grave sculpture of India, which was copied in China in stone but was reproduced in bronze in Japan. The trinity is not Japanese looking, but suggests Indian-Chinese Buddhist origins.

Many people agree that the greatest work of this early Buddhist period is the Miroku Bosatsu in the Chujuji nunnery near Nara. It is a wonderful figure of the Buddha of the Future, carved from wood. Probably it was once painted; but now the paint has all worn off, and the surface is so darkened by age that it looks as though it were made of metal. This figure reminds us of the *haniwa* because its lines are so simple and clear and it is so very natural. The seated image seems to be alive, expressing what we might describe as an idealized spirit of Buddhism, or inner harmony, peace, and contentment. The face is beautiful.

Chinese and Korean influences on Japanese sculpture are not hard to explain, nor is Indian; but it is surprising to find that sometimes even Greek touches turned up so far from home. Yet traders were carrying precious Chinese fabrics and spices across India and by sea right on to the Persian Gulf. Prince Shotoku had by now proclaimed Buddhism to be Japan's state religion and was giving his support to glorifying it. Any faraway influence affecting Buddhism in India can also be expected to appear in Japan.

Sculpture was the most important art form of the Nara period, which followed the times of Prince Shotoku. The sculptors used clay and lacquer as well as bronze and wood. This was Japan's China-dominated era. Artists and craftsmen went back and forth across the China Sea, praising the wonders of the T'ang court. Priests and statesmen, philosophers and traders, all wanted to visit the great Middle Kingdom, as China called herself.

Sculpture of this time took on a new manner of composition or arrangement. Smoothness and full, flowing lines appeared. Religious images were more human than they had been. Bronze casting techniques were also improved.

Again, an image at Horyuji is useful as an illustration. It is the Amida Trinity in the miniature shrine of Lady Tachibana, probably dating from about 710. It represents the pleasant Buddha, Amida, or the Buddha of Enduring Light, who was immensely popular in Japan. *Bodhisattvas*, or those who were becoming buddhas, are on either side of him, and all three are backed by a lacy screen. The seven Buddhas of the Past hover above the screen. Below, the souls of the blessed are seated on lotus flowers which symbolize Paradise. The angels who carry the souls of those about to die to rebirth in Paradise seem poised, ready to take wing at any moment. Every detail is touched with graceful movement. Tendrils and leaves of the lotus plants sway in a rising motion which begins with their roots and never stops until it ends with the happily reborn above. Flames rise from the halo behind the head of the central figure. The halo derives from worship of the sun. The use of the halo indicates Buddhism's similarity to a number of other religions that started with sun worship. This sculptured work gives one a wonderful feeling. Faces are serene, and the flowing lines of the robes suggest the Indian way of combining religious and physical beauty.

In 1937 the head of a bronze Buddha of Medicine was found at Kofukuji, one of the seven great temples of Nara. It is a fine example of a trend toward naturalism in religious sculpture. The lines of this head are dramatically strong and clear, and there is almost no detail. One could almost think that the Greeks had a hand in making it.

Although one could find many more bronze examples of the trend toward naturalism that was taking place in the Nara period, the best loved sculptural material of the time was not bronze but dry lacquer. This technique, like so many others, first appeared in China. While clay was easier to work with than wood, it was easily damaged. Lacquer, on the other hand, was light, tough, and almost indestructible.

Two ways of making lacquer sculpture were perfected. The first began with a solid, rough core of wood. Hemp cloth was stretched over this, and many coats of lacquer were added until a hard, smooth, plastic effect that gave the image gentle, rounded lines was achieved. The second method depended on a framework that supported the lacquer. It could be made of wood or of wire. Fabrics soaked in lacquer were molded over the frame and shaped as they dried, much as school children make papier-maché masks today, until the figures took on the form that was intended. A similar method was to start with a clay core which could later be dug out. Individual parts of a statue were sometimes made over clay molds. When dry, they were removed in sections and joined. In this case the joinings were covered with lacquer in the finishing process. But a solid core or a framework of wood seem to have been the most common methods.

Often the making of dry lacquer statues was a group undertaking which involved a carpenter, a painter or lacquer worker, and a designer. Here artistry showed most in the face. Bodies were almost always stiff and often quite alike, but the face could say a great deal when it was shaped and finished by sensitive fingers.

Images with more than the usual number of heads and arms also appeared in Japan in this period. This practice originated in India. Many heads suggested more wisdom, or more kinds of wisdom, in a god; many hands and arms meant generosity and willingness to help.

Among others, the Eleven-headed Kwannon of Shin-Yakushiji and the lively Ashura Deva, both at Nara, who have multiple heads and arms, delightfully express a new freedom. Their magical quality perhaps inspires belief beyond what seems possible. Ashura Deva is supposed to have been a Hindu demon king who became first a devout follower of Buddha and then one of his guardians. His skin is light red; his hair, dark red. Being a foreign god, he did not need to look Japanese. He is slim, boyish, almost a dancer.

In the Toshodai Temple at Nara stands a wooden statue of a thousand-headed Kwannon, eighteen feet high, with 953 of the heads still left. Beside it is a dry lacquer figure of Ganjin, a blind Chinese priest, said to have been made by his followers to honor him. Ganjin, who founded a particular Buddhist sect in Japan, was much revered during the eighth century. He was blind by the time he reached the Japanese islands, and the sculptor who portrayed him put such a feeling of blindness into his work that both the pose and the facial expression carry it vividly. This marvelous work is a splendid example of lacquer made over a wooden frame, or hollow lacquer. Portraying actual persons in sculpture may have grown from emphasizing facial expression. Sculpture tended to become more realistic as time passed and represented people as they were instead of idealizing them.

Masks can be thought of as portrait sculpture, too. They were worn with elegant costumes and came to be highly respected, particularly when they were part of the dress of the *bugaku* dancers. Some of the masks are intended to represent invading white men, such as long-nosed, red-faced traders, and are full of humor and satire.

During the Nara period clay, which had been used for the earliest sculpture, became popular again. The first step in this kind of work was to make a core of wood and to wrap it tightly with rice straw rope. Clay could be shaped and molded around this core. Dried clay sculpture lasted for centuries.

Sometimes only the secondary figures in a group were made of clay, while the central ones were bronze or wood. An example of this practice is the group of the Twelve Heavenly Generals which encircle the wooden Yakushi Buddha or Buddha of Medicine in the Shin-Yakushi Temple, Nara, near which the afore-mentioned Eleven-headed Kwannon also stands. These clay guardian figures are fierce-looking foreign warriors with bulging eyes, curly hair, and wild expressions. One of the Twelve Generals is portrayed roaring at his enemies. Even his hair joins the protest against them, standing out from his head like spikes.

By the ninth century dry lacquer and clay had been almost entirely replaced in statuary by wood. Even bronze was rare. In trying to explain this change, some people suggest that sandalwood images, which were by this time being imported, may have helped to start a fresh interest in wood sculpture. Sandalwood belongs to the myrtle family, and has a fine grain and a delicious odor. Although it still had to be imported from the Fiji Islands, the Chinese had long used it for fine boxes, for the framework of some of their best fans, and for incense. It was powdered to make incense, which gives out a spicy odor when it is burned.

In India sandalwood is also powdered to make the vermilion paste with which people touch their faces to indicate caste. It has also long been used for the cremation of important people in that country. When Gandhi was assassinated in 1948, his funeral pyre was laid with sandalwood.

Because of all these uses it is easy to see why religious images carved from this material would have a special appeal in the Far East. But there may be other important reasons why wooden sculpture became predominant in Japan in the ninth century. For one thing, Buddhism was so highly developed by this time that many images were needed. It was easy and cheap to make them of wood. Japan had a great deal of timber. Carving was simpler than constructing images of clay or lacquer.

But as time went on, Buddhist thinking changed and forced a change in its images, too. Buddha came to seem more sympathetic toward men, and the expression in his eyes became dreamy, gentle, and understanding. Even some of his followers who had often been represented as quite terrifying now seemed disinterested or even pleasant persons. A statue of the famous Prince Shotoku by Enkai, a renowned sculptor, in 1069 A.D., is realistic and yet has a Buddha-like calmness.

Jocho, who was a well-known sculptor of Enkai's time, joined separate pieces of wood to make his figures. This method allowed the sculptor to try out different poses without starting from the beginning each time, and increased the possible size of a work. Sculptors also discovered a new way of organizing themselves. Under a master they formed teams who specialized in some particular part of the image or job, a kind of mass production. Until this time sculptors were usually laymen or professional artisans employed by the government. But during this period, most sculptors were also priests connected with monasteries. Jocho was a priest and was awarded high Buddhist honors for his work, especially for the Amida Buddha at Hoodo. This beautiful image sits calmly before a halo made up of lively angels, strumming and piping musicians, sailing clouds, and rising flames.

Buddhist figures were usually male, but the Eleven-headed Kwannon of Shin-Yakushiji at Nara is female.

This figure shows that some time after the early Asuka and the later Nara periods, Buddhism began to include goddesses. This change probably came from China, for there Kuan-yin, the Goddess of Mercy, had become extremely important to ordinary people. She seemed more personal than the old Buddha and his dignified saints. But this feeling of closeness to the female Buddhist image does not seem so important in Japan, perhaps because the two peoples are quite different. Because of Confucianism, there was great emphasis on the family in China. All parents hoped for sons who would carry on the family name and prayed to the Goddess of Mercy for a male child. Perhaps Chinese felt freer to show their anxiety about children than the Japanese because for centuries the Japanese had had a strict social code about suitable behavior which meant that they often had to hide their real feelings. In China it was expected that a woman who had no son would weep aloud before Kuan-yin and throw baby shoes into her merciful hands while friends and relatives looked on with sympathy and admiration. But in Japan prayers were restrained and formal, and if anyone made a public prayer those who passed would be likely to avert their eyes. Even this difference may not explain the variation between the feelings of the two peoples for this friendly goddess.

When the next great step in history came and the Fujiwara clan moved the capital to Kamakura to get it away from the soft, religious luxury of Kyoto, dramatic change set in. The Kamakura period (1186–1335) is the most important of all in the story of Japanese sculpture. Famous leaders full of fresh inspiration gave it size, vigor, and realism.

What was happening among the Japanese people to make this so? The civil wars that led to the change of capital had destroyed many of the beautiful buildings in Nara, yet Buddhism still patronized the arts and encouraged the rebuilding of ruined monasteries and temples. Artists turned to realism to express better their feelings to ordinary people and to military men who had left the luxuries of Nara as well as Kyoto for the fishing village of Kamakura. Even in China, the Sung court was beginning to represent Buddhism in everyday terms.

Kokei was the leader of the group of artists known as the Nara sculptors. One of his six sculptor sons, Unkei, and a pupil, Kaikei, worked with him. The three were entrusted with restoring two of the great Buddhist centers, Kofukuji and Todaiji between 1180 and 1212 A.D. They could still appreciate the magnificence that these places had had back in the eighth century, and they set to work under that inspiration.

The result was a combination of the grandeur of Nara and the realism of Kamakura.

The two Nio, or guardian kings, which stand at the south gate of the Todaiji show what this combination meant. Carved of wood, and now cracked with age, the twenty-six foot figures are alive, threatening, full of power, and ready to spring forward. Their poses, the tension of their taut muscles in arms, chests, shoulders, and abdomen, and the looks in their faces all express life. Figures of Kuya-Shonin preaching, of Basu Sennin, an attendant of Buddha, of Shoko-o, one of the kings of hell, all demonstrate the realism which marked the Unkei school. Often something in the statue appears so familiar that we feel we have met the person represented.

The Great Buddha of Kamakura, which every tourist tries to see, belongs to this age of ambitious military leaders, of Mongol invasions which the gods themselves seemed to stop, and of dramatic art forms in other fields. It is made of bronze and stands forty-nine feet high including the dais. It was once housed in a temple; but since that was destroyed by fire or a tidal wave, it stands in the open. It has the placid Amida Buddha expression except for an odd moustache which shows, some people say, that Buddha was of foreign origin.

The trend toward portrait sculpture became so strong during the Kamakura period that it continued into the sixteenth century. When wars broke out at this unsettled time, Zen monasteries were the cultural centers. Scholars and artists went there for refuge. But sculpture slowly became less important than painting in these quiet courts. Beautiful ink painting, which could so well interpret man's inward thoughts, became one of the greatest arts.

Still, sculpture never stops, and Japan's folk sculpture is rich and varied. Masks have already been mentioned in connection with a special dance. They are common in many connections. Dolls, too, are common, and every village—almost every home—has at least one of some kind. One doll that has been popular for centuries and is still to be found in most market places is *Daruma*, named for the sage who brought Zen Buddhism to China from India. He was said to be so devout that he sat meditating for ten years and as a result entirely lost the use of his legs. Daruma dolls are legless and rounded at the bottom. They are often made of papier-maché and gaily painted.

Other varieties of folk sculpture can be found all over Japan. Though clay or wood, lacquer or bronze are the mediums of Japan's true sculpture, wayside images of Dosojin, the god of roads and happy marriages, and of Jizo, who helps travelers, are cut from coarse lava stone. Jizo is also the special protector of children and mothers. Often his shrines are covered with the clothing of little children who have died. Childless women sometimes go to Sado Island to throw small stone images of Jizo into the sea as an offering. These images are not much more than cylinders topped with a head and folded hands cut in shallow relief. They remind one of the *haniwa* and are appealing for the same reasons.

Graveyards and temples are full of small statues and carvings of familiar likenesses of Buddha and his followers. Most of them were probably copies from images at Nara. Sometimes these copies are more powerful than the originals because part of the details have been left out and the main lines are clearer. Many are cut on rock faces in relief.

Folk sculpture shows the Japanese touch especially well because it does not have to follow artistic rules. Like many everyday things in Japan, it is interesting because it is simple.

7

Tints and Textures

A visitor to Japan soon notices the textiles. Even though western dress is common now, brilliant *kimono* of all sizes, splendid outer coats with family insignia and crests, waving flags, and undulating banners along busy market streets are vivid. A peasant bringing his enormous white radishes to town or a woman peddling toys will probably be dressed in a garment of coarse cotton, but it is almost certainly decorated with a *batik* design astonishing in its simplicity.

I will never forget a Japanese fish woman who climbed to our little summer cottage near Nagasaki one hot summer morning to sell us some of her catch. She was fresh looking and rosy-cheeked. Her heavy black hair had escaped the pins intended to hold it in place. She wore an everyday *kimono* of some white material which was decorated with a few gray crabs and a red lobster or two. These were softened by a wisp of seaweed entangled in a lobster's claws. The woman seemed to have stepped out of a breaking surf, *kimono*, basket, fish, and all, as well designed as a modern abstraction and yet perfectly natural.

Mists of legend hide the early part of the story of textiles in Japan. After weaving was introduced from China early in the Christian era it was carried on in Yamato, the first cultural center of the islands, where Emperor Jimmu established himself. Later, Yamato people learned from Korean immigrants how to raise mulberry trees to feed silkworms and how to produce their own silk.

When Buddhism reached Japan, Nara sent weaving experts out through the provinces or townships to teach the art. They experimented with dyes using many different roots combined with vinegar and wood ash.

Marsh grass and wild orange produced blues and greens; jasmine resulted in yellow. Some silks dyed by these ancient processes have held their colors for more than a thousand years. But while these materials were being woven and dyed, brocades and satins and fine silks for important princes and priests were being imported from the mainland because the best homemade silks had to be used for tribute to the Chinese court.

One reason that the history of textiles is hard to follow is that such materials are perishable. Samples from early times are usually just not to be found. Although we know what the court costumes of the ninth and tenth centuries were like from literary descriptions of them, none of them are any longer in existence. They are described as very delicate in texture, often of one solid color with little decoration. We can see from paintings of the time that court ladies wore the "twelve-layer" costume made of garments of different hues worn over a full skirt and tied at the waist. Variation in men's clothes seemed to come by using undergarments of contrasting shades and letting the edges peep out at the sleeves and at the lower edges of their flowing robes, which hung down over baggy trousers.

All this seemed to go with a court life that was highly refined and put great emphasis on small points of etiquette. A great deal of romance went on, and court ladies wrote long diaries and novels about it. The most famous novel, *Genji Monogatari*, or *The Tale of Genji*, describes many court scenes. This shortened quotation from a translation by Arthur Waley gives a glimpse of court dress:

Part of the race course was not far away from this side of the palace, and a good view could be obtained from the portico and outer galleries, which soon were thronged. Persons of quality were hidden behind green shutters or curtains dyed in the new-fashioned way, with color running down into the fringe. Among the dresses of the visitors were many elaborate Chinese costumes especially designed for the day's festivity, the color of the young dianthus leaf tending to prevail. Some were in their summer gowns, green without and peach-blossom color within. There was a great deal of rivalry and self-display, which was rewarded from time to time by a glance from one of the young courtiers who were assembled on the course.

Genji arrived on the scene at the hour of the sheep (1 p.m.). It was interesting to see the competitors, so differently arrayed, each with his following of smartly dressed squires and assistants. The sports continued until evening. The ladies, though understanding very imperfectly what was going on, were at least capable of *deriving a great deal of pleasure from the sight of so many young men in elegant riding jackets hurling themselves with desperate recklessness into the fray.**

When Zen Buddhist influence grew strong during the next era, clothing was affected by it. There are some samples of dress from this period in certain Shinto shrines. Materials were of the finest quality; but colors were subdued, and patterns or decorations were simple.

During the twelfth, thirteenth, and fourteenth centuries of the Kamakura period when the great military leaders were in power, textiles again reflected the spirit of the times, as did ceramics and sculpture. Short-sleeved *kimono* worn next to the skin allowed much freer movement than many-layered flowing garments. Texture and design were still important, but now they were altogether unlike what they had been during the two periods before this. Weaves were fine, and motifs were harshly realistic. Dyes were very cleverly applied on some of the *kimono* worn by the dictators. An outer coat, which was designed for Hideyoshi and probably worn by him is dyed in two colors; purple over the

---

* Lady Murasaki, *The Tale of Genji*, tr. by Arthur Waley, Houghton-Mifflin, Boston, 1935. Shortened as in Marion May Dilts, *The Pageant of Japanese History*, Second Edition, Longmans, Green, London, New York, Toronto, 1947.

shoulders and below the knees, and green in between. A stenciled decoration made up of arrows and of paulownia twigs showing leaves and blossoms is thrown against these vivid backgrounds. The paulownia is used in two ways, one for each background color, while the arrows point sharply downward from the purple border, only their feathered ends decorating the space.

When *Noh* plays became popular, they inspired still other ideas in textiles. Designs were still simple, but they were used dramatically. Colored silk was sometimes combined with gold and silver foil. In the up-and-down halves of a garment a small neat pattern might be combined with a large, bold design. The sleeve would match the half of the body on the other side rather than that adjacent to it, making a kind of balance of opposites.

Although Kyoto became the heart of the textile craft through the sixteenth, seventeenth, and eighteenth centuries, other centers of weaving sprang up. Styles became more and more gorgeous. New ways of dyeing introduced interesting changes. One of these was *Yuzen,* a process which a priest of that name originated. The design is marked out in rice flour paste or in wax to keep the dye from taking, so that it is left uncolored against a colored background. Sometimes designs are combined with tie-dyeing or with embroidery, which may include gold or silver thread. Yuzen dyed silks are still a specialty of Kyoto, where they were developed so long ago. Craftsmen who make these silks gathered in a section of a city called Nishijin. As time passed the finest cloths were so heavily covered with decorations that their textures were entirely hidden.

Today a number of ancient ways of decorating cloth as well as designs from nearby countries are being reproduced in the folk arts.

The small, desolate island of Okinawa has played an important part in Japanese textiles. Because of its location, Okinawa was influenced by powerful neighboring

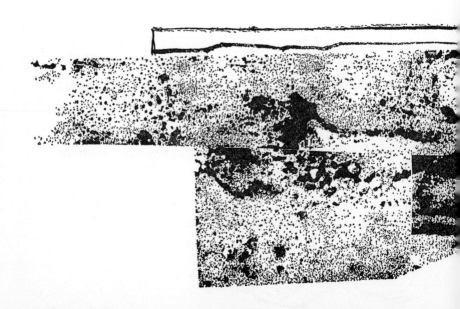

states. It was under the domination of one or another of them most of the time, so that it had to pay tribute. This tribute was traditionally paid in textiles; but such tribute was not acceptable unless the materials were of fine quality. The Okinawans had to find more and more expert ways of weaving and dyeing.

The *kasuri* or "scattered design," which originated with the wall paintings of the Ajanta Caves in India, reached Japan by way of Java, Borneo, the Philippine Islands, and Okinawa. In its present form it is made up of abstract geometrical designs, but these still show that they came from the Ajanta Caves.

Today the most attractive Okinawa fabrics are stencil-dyed ones known as *bingata*, or colored patterns. On the island, the social status of the wearer can be told by the design of his *kimono* material. Bold designs are usually reserved for the nobility or first families. Colors also have a status value. Yellow is the royal one. Sometimes designs show where they came from. Those that came from China are probably the most easily identified. Again, designs mean certain things. One delightful pattern uses butterflies and dragonflies to stand for the spirits of the dead.

Besides the *kasuri* and *bingata*, there is a third common Okinawa design of stripes and plaids. Though the patterns are sober, contrasts between pastels and bril-

liant reds, yellows, blues, and browns are rich and
pleasing. Many modern textile patterns have been
inspired by the fabrics of this small island.

A traditional cloth which is still being produced in
Japan itself is called *tamba*. This was first made famous
in the district of the same name. It was used as a covering material for Japanese bedding, or quilts, known as
futon. The texture of *tamba* is soft and thick, for it is
woven with a woof of undyed silk waste and a warp of
cotton. This results in an irregular weave which has a
rough but not a harsh texture. Although *tamba* cloth
is now dyed mechanically, its colors are still very like
the original clear blues, soft browns, and black.

Two other types of cloth that are especially attractive are also of ancient origin. The first, *kazuki*, was
woven for women to wear over their heads whenever
they left their homes. It originated in Kyoto and then
was produced in the Shonai district of Yamata Prefecture. In modern times it is worn only at funerals.
While it used to be woven of fine silk, it is now of
coarse hemp, perhaps because of its connection with
mourning. Though the colors are somber, designs are
sometimes bold.

The second cloth, *kogin*, comes from Tohoku, an
area in the beautiful northeastern mountains sometimes called the Tohoku Alps. This pattern is a lovely,

clear-cut one made by embroidering indigo linen with white thread in such a way that it actually looks as if it were woven. The embroidery usually covers the back or the upper front of garments. Families have traditional patterns and hand down decorated garments from one generation to another. They are worn at festive functions and treasured as family heirlooms.

Still another type of embroidery cloth is *e-kasuri*. Perhaps it is related to the scattered designs of the Okinawa *kasuri* already mentioned. This is really small pictures—*e-* means picture—worked on indigo cloth with white thread. Farm folk first did this kind of embroidery during the winter, when they could not work outdoors. They often used good luck symbols like cranes or tortoises. Sometimes they turned to designs like pines, carp, bamboos, cocks, birds, or Mount Fuji, which are also typical of Japan. While machine goods have replaced many of the lovely hand-woven materials of Japan, except as folk art revivals have kept some of them in production, the Japanese sense of design has not changed. Space is still as important as what fills it. Colors and subjects need follow no fixed ideas as to how they should be combined or chosen.

In what other country would one find a crab or a lobster placed in such a wide setting of sand or sea that one's eye has to cross an entire garment to find its balancing wisp of seaweed? Where else would one think of waves—*only* waves—for a design; or only clouds; or a pair of wooden sandals or *geta*; or a narrow-mouthed fishbasket; or a lantern; or a single branch of bamboo; or a cast iron kettle and a pair of tongs; or an open umbrella; or three reeds swaying in marshy water? Nowhere but in Japan.

While many priceless ceremonial robes make a splendid display, their beauty is, in a way, not as typical of Japan as a flowered curtain which shuts off the back passage of a village shop or restaurant or the folded *futon* in a simple home or the bright *kimono* of a child holding the hand of his mother, followed by the dull hues of his grandmother, or the waving banners in a market place. The colors in the clothing of a family in native garb out to view the cherry trees is like the pallet of an artist, with splashes of vividness set artlessly against the beauty of nature.

Once I was given a roll of narrow silk. It was *obi* cloth intended to be used for the broad sash of the traditional Japanese dress. It had been woven on a hand loom and was a rich red decorated only with a neat white and black geometric pattern. Its texture was heavy; its color luxurious so that only a touch of design was needed. It was a sample of Japanese textiles at their best.

8

Bamboo and Basketry, Paper and Thatch

The Japanese gift for finding what is beautiful in the everyday things of home life shows especially in their use of bamboo. Even though bamboo is practical and useful, it has a mystery about it, a fairy tale quality that it never altogether loses.

Its smooth, green stalks and the slick carpet of dry leaves under them that chokes out any other growth give a grave, strange, eerie feeling. Because its shoots pierce hard ground and dart skyward toward the sun, sometimes at the rate of a foot in twenty-four hours, it is unique in the world's vegetation, and this fact adds to its mystery.

As a child I heard stories about criminals who had been punished by being fastened to the ground in bamboo groves so that growing shoots would pierce their bodies. Perhaps, too, because the throbbing bell of a Buddhist temple sounded from the depths of a dark patch of bamboos on the shady side of the hill where I lived, bamboos will always seem to be hiding some secret from me. To the Westerner bamboo, more than any other material, represents the East.

We usually think of bamboo as a wood, but it really belongs to the grass family. About five hundred varieties of bamboo are native to Africa, Asia, and South, Central, and North America. Bamboo also does well when cultivated in some parts of Europe. It is an extraordinarily valuable plant, useful in an infinite variety of ways. Tender shoots of some varieties are used as foods; the hulls which drop from thick shoots as they emerge from the ground serve as stiffening in making soles for cloth-topped shoes or as waterproofing in bamboo-framed rain hats. Mature bamboo trunks or stems can be used for everything from the construction of houses to the delicate ribs of fragile fans. For bamboo comes in many sizes, varying from a slender, grassy stalk with little more than aesthetic value in a dish garden to a trunk three feet in circumference. Giant bamboos may grow to be more than one hundred feet high. Such a stalk when cut with the joints of its sections in mind serves as a perfect bucket with a handle. Smaller varieties, properly cut and furnished with a long stick handle, are excellent dippers. When the joints have been cut or burnt through from the inside, trunks can be used for pipes, one small end being fitted into the large end of the next, to convey water a long way from its source. Many rural bridges are constructed of bamboo; and though these are often unsteady and sway in a terrifying fashion, they are strong and durable. Experiments are being made in reinforcing concrete with bamboo instead of steel. Cables are made of split and interwoven bamboo; while stools, chairs, tables, fences, and screens are commonly made of this material in many parts of the Orient. Bamboo becomes very hard when it dries, so that it serves as wood or even as metal.

Small varieties of bamboo are good for weaving mats and for making cages, handles for paintbrushes or brush pens, and fishing rods of all kinds. When bamboo is crushed to a pulp, it produces a fine paper.

Yet this list of the uses of bamboo is still incomplete. Archaeological findings show that the Japanese were making bamboo baskets three thousand years ago. As time went on the baskets varied to suit their changing uses. Many styles have been traditionally connected with certain localities. Such baskets often combine woven patterns with symmetrical shapes in most pleasing ways, and yet they are made to be used. Fish baskets, salt containers, trays or flat baskets, and nests of baskets are ordinary utensils. But however menial their purpose, they are usually decorated by a touch of contrast, perhaps only a darker shade in the binding strip around the edge or a single slip circling like a stripe. Other bamboo household objects are such things as whisks or brooms, dippers or cups, and, most indispensable of all, chopsticks. It is hard to resist the beauty of bamboo in Japan. Its texture, its shape, and even its soft, neutral colors are attractive.

Bamboo is used for the framework of umbrellas, lanterns, lamps, fans, and kites, too. These are beautiful in a fragile way. The ordinary Japanese umbrella, made of paper drawn over a slender but sturdy framework and then thoroughly oiled and left in its natural color or dyed has its own charm. On a rainy day, a Japanese street full of swaying umbrellas and the regular tapping sound of high, wooden *geta* on glistening cobblestones provides a real experience of beauty. Japanese artists have been sensitive to this beauty, as we shall see, and have found the view of a single figure leaning to keep its balance in the wind and slanting rain or caught in a field of jostling umbrellas a sight so entrancing that all the world has come to appreciate it through their eyes.

Lanterns, whether they are for festivals or for use on a moist, windy night or a belated dawn, or whether they are modernistic lamps with electric fittings, are charming too. A lantern that bobs down a street at the end of a stick held in someone's hand, reflecting light from every door lintel, stone guardian figure, over-hanging tree, or approaching rickshaw, seems almost alive. Its soft rays change everything they touch, cloth-ing ordinary objects in mystery. Such a lantern can speak a language all its own when it is lifted to light up a passing face—a face that stares back blankly or breaks into smiles of recognition.

What a comfort a slender bamboo-ribbed fan can be on a hot day! Fans were used long ago in the dignified parades of Egyptian Pharaohs and in Rome. In Old Testament stories we read of their blowing chaff from wheat in winnowing. The Chinese used fans two thousand years before Christ. The first fans seem to have been palm leaves. Then artisans copied the natural palm leaf and made ribs of thin wood, bamboo, ivory, or silver and covered them with silk or paper for fans. Later, they cleverly designed folding fans, which were in common use in China long before they were introduced in Europe during the Crusades. It is easy to imagine that they appeared in Japan when other useful articles were imported from China.

Fans are often made for some special person and may carry the emblems of a noble family. They are also often suited to a type of person. Those for women of leisure, for instance, are likely to be delicate, fragrant, and decorated in traditional patterns. Those for housewives or working girls need to be sturdier, but bright and pretty. Grandmothers' fans are usually subdued in color and design. Men's fans are generally conservative to suit their dark *kimono*. They are not now used by men in public as commonly as they once were, but they are part of the native costume a man dons to make himself comfortable for the evening when the workday is over.

Many fans are works of art. Their frames are beautifully carved out of bone or ivory or sandalwood, and they are covered with fine silk or beautiful paper. The paper is painted by the skilled hand of an artist, and the silk may be painted or embroidered in tiny designs or scenes. Sometimes poetry inscribed by an expert calligrapher is combined with a painting; sometimes writing is the full decoration. The painting of fans came to be one of the specialized water color arts.

Folding fans are often connected with music and dancing and with other delicate graces of the Japanese in our minds. The sturdy non-folding fan with its traditional palm-leaf shape, gaily decorated, is an essential item in any Japanese household; almost a utensil. In modern times folk artists are producing interesting utility fans decorated with stencil designs.

Kites have been made in both China and Japan for hundreds of years. In both countries kite flying became a highly skilled sport. Competitions in cutting down kites as they soar by crossing their flying ropes, which have been covered with ground glass, have become annual events in Japan. Naruto City, which stands on the mile-wide channel connecting the Inland Sea with the Pacific Ocean between the small island of Awaji and the large one of Shikoku, is famous for its kite-flying festival. It was first celebrated two hundred years ago and is held in July and August, when the winds are strongest. More than one thousand kites are flown, and some are said to be as much as fifty feet in diameter and to weigh several thousand pounds. Nagasaki also has a kite-flying festival. When a kite takes off into the sky, whether it is a giant held by as many as two hundred men or a toy shaped like an animal or a flower and flown by a child, it is beautiful.

In addition to all the practical ways bamboo is used in both China and Japan, it is a subject of art in both countries. This is not surprising, because bamboo expresses many different things. Bamboos seem stark and strong when they stand perfectly still, upright and without any low out-branchings. The shade beneath them is dark. Again, a grove of bamboo on a mountain side is like oversize ferns which caress the slope, swaying in the wind with a flowing motion. When snow falls on bamboo, it collects in layers on the evergreen leaves in pure beauty.

Bamboo is one of the most important themes of Japanese painting. It is also a design used for lacquer, wrought iron, and textiles. Pottery and porcelain are decorated with a single branch or even a few leaves. The shadow of bamboo as it is thrown on a screen, or a group of shoots, tawny red before their sheaths are dropped, are highly ornamental.

Many other varieties of the grass family influence art and add beauty to everyday utensils in the Japanese home. Thatched roofs are astonishingly durable as well as beautiful. Thatch may cover a peasant home or a cherished shrine, for thatch is one of the oldest building materials and is especially suited to Shintoism because it is simple and close to nature. It seems to be part of a landscape. Thatch used for the roof of such a structure as the ancient shrine at Ise is expertly laid. The thickness of the thatch increases as it approaches the eaves and is then trimmed, as if by a giant razor blade, in a concave curve under the overhanging edge. This line takes one delightfully by surprise.

Buddhist temples as well as Shinto shrines were often covered with thatch. It seemed to suit the rich decorations of Buddhist buildings and many of the great palaces of military lords as well, perhaps because it is plain and massive. But Japanese peasant homes and farmhouses with thatch roofs are particularly appealing, for beauty seems accidental there.

Thatch roofs vary in style. There are gabled roofs and hipped roofs. There are even four-storied houses under one great thatch roof. In such a building the lower floor has generally been used for silkworm culture while the workers, who may number up to fifty, are quartered in the rooms above. The more typical farmhouse has only one floor, and its roof may be thatch or tile. Combined wood and lattice shutters and, in some areas, plaster walls, give beautiful contrast to the dark roof. Carefully laid thatch seems to protect itself from the weather and lasts a long time. Such a roof with wide eaves offers a strip of shade in the summer and a windbreak in winter.

Thatch is not only used as a building material. Peasant rain or sun hats are often made of a kind of thatch, and rain capes are of grass. These capes are cheap and practical, for they are light and shed water amazingly well. The most famous ones come from Honshu. They are woven tight at the neck, and are sometimes embroidered with colored thread so as to have a patterned yoke.

The great artist Hiroshige liked to make wood-block prints of rain. Nothing seemed to express the mood of rain or the feeling of moist winds as well as a figure clutching a rain cape tightly about itself, head bent low toward the storm so that the wind could not snatch off the grass rain hat and so that the water would be shed at the best angle; the marvelous paper umbrellas that seemed to come alive as he created them. We find delightful examples of his use of rain. In "Fujieda" a man on horseback is entirely enveloped in his rain cape, while another is huddling beneath his on the ground; still others of the group are protecting themselves as well as they can. In "The Fifty-three Stages of the Tokaido" one finds a wonderful scene where travelers are fighting wind and rain on a mountain side; trees are whipped by the storm, and figures are bent double, while thatch-roofed farmhouses cling to the mountain slope below the road. There is another lovely example in the same series of prints, "Tsuchiyama," where men are struggling against snow and rain. The simple grass outfit of a Japanese peasant on a wet day is charming. Even brooms, straw snow shoes, and sun hats display graceful handicraft that is most pleasing.

Tatami, the finely woven rush mats which are the usual covering of floors in Japanese homes, are attractive for their soft, neutral shades, their resilience when one walks on them, and their textured weaving. They have appealed to the Japanese artist, too, and one often finds them adding color and atmosphere to paintings of interiors.

Not only bamboo and straw and rushes are used to make articles that are practical as well as beautiful. Vines and bark shape baskets and other carrying utensils. Ingenuity and clever fingers often produce what no other people would think of making.

For many centuries paper has been very important in Japanese life. It is combined with bamboo to make many of the things we have been discussing, such as umbrellas, lanterns and lamps, fans and kites. It is used to cover sliding doors or *fusuma* and paper screens, *shoji*, which are the inner divisions in a Japanese home. Tough paper is pasted on light wooden frames to make them.

Paper is made in a number of different ways and from several materials—bark, grasses, rice straw, and sometimes silk waste or cotton. Although paper was once thought to have been invented by the Arabs and brought to Asia during their travels, explorers in the early twentieth century discovered that paper was known in China as early as 150 A.D. It must have reached Japan at the same time as other cultural materials. Before much time had passed, the Japanese were expert in the art of paper making and soon became famous for it.

Fine quality handmade paper can be produced only by great skill and patience. Some Japanese villages make it by age-old processes, for Japan still makes the finest papers of the world. The white bark of the *kozo*, a kind of mulberry tree, is the best material for Japanese paper, but the barks of several other trees and shrubs are also used. Some areas are known for their papers. These usually have some unique quality of texture or shade. Even though much of Japan's paper is manufactured by machinery today, its handmade products still far surpass any of these.

Superior paper is necessary for water colors and for the fine prints that have had such an important part in the arts of Japan. Fine paper suggests beauty in its own texture and sheen. It can be the stuff of art when it covers an umbrella, a lantern, or a fan; it participates in the work of a master when it provides the background of a painting or when, left empty, it gives a sense of quiet space. The ruggedness of coarse brown paper is attractive too, enhancing colors because it is so neutral. Its texture makes one feel that the stalks of which it is made have been scarcely more than crushed, rolled, or beaten into the form it has. So paper is not only useful but also beautiful in itself.

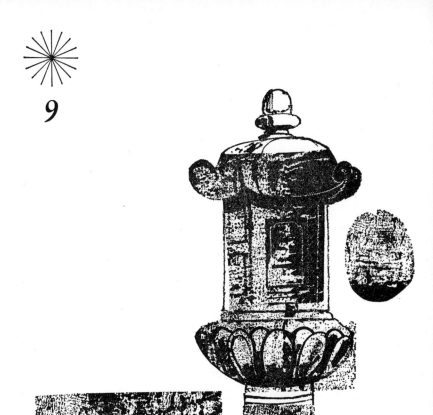

9

Precious Gardens

When the screens or wooden walls of a Japanese house have been pushed aside or taken down, the garden becomes a part of the house. One can almost say that it is the most important part, because the Japanese let their imaginations go when it comes to their gardens. Because their gardens mean very much to them, they sometimes seem quite reckless in spending money to get a desired effect.

The idea of landscaped gardens originated in China and reached Japan from Korea. By the fifth century they were included in architectural plans for imperial palaces. By the Heian period (782–1185 A.D.) they usually lay to the south of the buildings. These great gardens featured ponds or lakes that were connected with the rest of the property by artistic bridges. Artificial hills often suggested distance and variety and sometimes provided a view.

There are two general types of gardens; level and hill. Hill gardens include artificial hills, a small stream with a waterfall, and a lake or a pond. Level gardens usually suggest a valley or moor by the way rocks are arranged or by a winding dry stream bed which gives an illusion of water. Sometimes hill gardens and level gardens are combined.

The relationship between house and garden is always important. Since the approach to the house from the garden affects this, it is usually planned to be on a curve or half hidden by sleeve fences. These are short fences attached to the sides of the house facing the garden, which both conceal some portions of the house and relate it to the garden.

The approach to the garden from the house, on the

other hand, is an even more serious matter. The garden is truly planned as an outdoor living room, and there is much more feeling connected with it in Japan than in the West. When the screens are pushed back to reveal the garden, space, trees, rocks, lights, and shadows all participate in the life of the house itself. Every tree, rock, stone lantern, *torii*, or miniature pagoda has been placed to harmonize indoors and outdoors. Even when the garden is tiny this is so. Japanese gardens do not have a vivid luxuriance of flower beds and wide lawns like those of America and Europe. They are controlled works of art that suggest space, give an illusion of craggy mountains by their weatherbeaten evergreens, and imply contrasts in nature by dark shadows thrown on white sand. The weathered rocks, seaside pebbles, and trees that have been so carefully chosen for this spot, often at great expense, add to the feeling of closeness to the whole universe. This studied design intends to reveal beauty and to suggest repose and meditation rather than simply to make a pretty place. Philosophy, if not religious feeling, lies behind it.

Garden arrangements are based on many different ideas. One may try to give the impression of a distant vista when there is actually only a small space; or of a cliff or a sandy beach or a wooded knoll when the city is rising on all sides and the garden is postage stamp size. Lafcadio Hearn, one of the most famous writers about Japan, says in one of his books:

I have been watching two old men planting young trees in the garden of a neighboring temple. They sometimes spend nearly an hour in planting a single sapling. Having fixed it in the ground, they retire to a distance to study the position of all its lines and consult together about it. As a consequence, the sapling is taken up and replanted in a slightly different position. This is done no less than eight times before the little tree can be perfectly adjusted into the plan of the garden. Those two old men are composing a mysterious thought with their little trees, changing them, transferring them, removing or replacing them, even as a poet changes and shifts his words, to give his verse the most delicate or the most forcible expression possible.*

Sometimes a home builder will pay what seems to be an outrageous price for a single tree or a few rocks for his garden. But to him and his sympathetic friends, and to the sensitive visitor, this single item may

---

* Lafcadio Hearn, *Out of the East*, Bernhard Tauchnitz, Leipzig, 1910, pp. 105, 106.

make the garden a success and have enormous influence on his home.

When Zen Buddhism became important in the Kamakura period between 1186 and 1335 A.D. it strongly influenced gardens. Two special things happened. Gardens increased their symbolism and took on a touch of mystery, and the ceremony of tea drinking introduced the teahouse.

Under the Zen influence rocks were examined for their shapes, colors, textures, and origins, not only to be sure that they were beautiful but also to be sure that they would convey the right feeling when they were in a garden. Spaces were painstakingly planned. Trees were shaped and planted to add just the right significance. *Torii*, although of Shinto origin, sometimes seemed right. The native sense of beauty that was so strong in the Japanese personality was clearer than ever seen through Zen. I have seen a Zen garden made of irregular stepping stones crossing sanded space, with nothing to soften it but the shadow of one pine tree.

The introduction of teahouses affected gardens even more obviously. They became important when the military dictators built them in their gardens. Teahouses are traditionally small, thatched-roofed houses made to look as rustic as possible and usually partially concealed by trees or bushes. They are approached by a path that is intended to cut them off from the world. The tearoom is only four and one half *tatami* in size, and one enters by a door so low that it is called the "wriggling-in entrance." It is made tiny so that all the

guests who come will seem to be of the same social standing, since they are leaving their worldly positions outside. These small houses came to have great prestige as time passed, for they stressed the love, almost the worship, of nature, and refined the formalities of Zen-influenced tea drinking.

Of course not every Japanese house can have a garden, however small. When there is no garden, a dish garden or flower arrangements are substituted. Dish gardens or "tray landscapes" are miniature gardens. They are cleverly arranged on a flat dish or some tray-like utensil. Peat, sand, soil, or even soaked paper may be used as a base in which tiny, carefully trained trees, moss, or other small plants are rooted, while pebbles and stones, miniature porcelain bridges, and teahouses complete the scene. The effect created in this way can be charming and can even suggest distance and space surprisingly well.

Dwarf trees are used in these tray landscapes. Growing and dwarfing such trees is an art; for miniature trees take more expert handling than full sized ones, since they have to be "dieted" so as not to grow too large and yet not die from the treatment they are given. They are shaped and twisted in order to appear ancient. Their minute roots are trained over rocks; trunks are made to lean, and branches to spread as if beaten by storms, and yet they are often less than a foot high. Sometimes ornamental trees are not put into miniature gardens but are planted in earthenware pots chosen for their shapes. Such a pot may hold a single tree or a small grove of well-trained ones. This variation of a dish garden sometimes looks lovely in an alcove or *tokonoma* or by an entrance.

Sand and stone tray arrangements are another form of dish garden. These are said to have begun when beautiful, rare, and oddly shaped stones from China were presented to Empress Suiko, who lived in the seventh century. At first these stones were just laid on trays to be admired. Later, sand was added to suggest a beach or a stream bed or a winding pathway between overhanging rocks, and they became miniature landscapes. Stones were chosen on the basis of what they suggested or for their poetic meanings. Greenish stones stood for spring; black ones, for summer; white ones, for winter; red ones, for autumn. Often "islands" in an "ocean" or "lake" were semiprecious stones, or crystal. Sometimes paste was mixed with sand so that the landscape could be molded. Again, real water and rock were placed in a tray and actual moss was encouraged to grow. This was called a "water and stone" arrangement. Such old techniques are still used.

Sand is extremely important in stone arrangements.

Different kinds of brushes, some no larger than a single feather, are used to sweep fine sand in particular ways. For example, where sand is used to simulate water in a shore scene, it must be so brushed as to suggest the way rollers break on the shore and how they are affected by jutting rocks or by inlets. These tray landscapes became very popular in connection with ceremonial tea drinking.

The tea ceremony had a great deal to do with arranging flowers formally. What came to be called "Flower Arrangement" grew out of a simple love of flowers. Moreover, emphasis on nature is part of Shintoism; Buddhists often decorated their altars with flowers; and finally Zen Buddhism made the use of flowers a cult. By the seventeenth century schools of flower arrangement had been started and were competing for popularity. Girls' schools included, and still include, courses in this special subject. Teachers of *ikebana* travel around the world, and learners flock to them.

A basic plan or theory lies behind the techniques of flower arrangement. A tall spray represents "the leading principle," or heaven. A low spray stands for "the subordinate principle," or earth. Between them is a third element to reconcile heaven and earth; it is man. There should always be these three elements, carefully related to each other, whatever else may be added. The season of the year and the association of the flowers with other items in the *tokonoma*, especially whatever scroll is hanging there, must be kept in mind as one works.

The care that was given to the art of arranging flowers made the results we know. Japanese feeling expressed in this way appealed to many people.

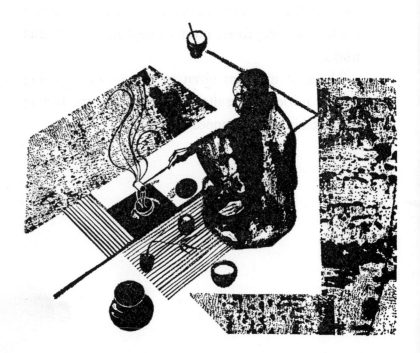

10

Simple Tea Turns Ceremonial

The pale amber drink that the West knows as green tea, one form of the world's most widely used beverage, plays an important part in Japanese life.

Tea leaves probably first reached Japan during the time of the T'ang dynasty in China. In 805 a Japanese priest named Saicho, who had been studying in China, brought some tea seeds with him when he came home. These were planted at Mt. Hiei near Kyoto.

The first time that tea was used formally seems to have been at a party that Emperor Shomu, of Nara times, gave for a hundred or so monks. When Emperor Kwammu, who moved the court from Nara to Kyoto, tasted tea in a monastery one day, he liked it so well that he ordered it to be cultivated throughout the islands.

The Japanese monk, Eisai, returning from a trip to China, prescribed tea for the son of the great Japanese military leader, Minamoto Yorimoto, to cure him of his drunkenness. Eisai had brought fine tea and tea seeds with him, and he started a special tea garden in the grounds of a temple near the old capital, Kyoto, which had been displaced by Kamakura. What was grown in this garden became the standard by which all tea was judged for its quality. Eisai wrote a classic essay on the healthful values of tea.

Fine tea leaves put in attractive jars easily became appropriate gifts for special friends as time went on. Officials sometimes rewarded those who served them well with such a present. One invited his close friends to enjoy the tea with him. Such tea drinking became a rather special occasion.

A Zen priest named Shuko took up this idea in the

fifteenth century and made it into a kind of ceremony.
He loved beautiful pottery and painting and wanted to
encourage an appreciation of them in others. He was a
collector of Chinese art. He began to serve tea in beautiful utensils in a small, spotlessly clean room where
only a miniature landscape broke the emptiness. Surely
monks who drank tea and meditated in such an atmosphere would love beauty more and more. Shogun
Yoshimasa patronized Shuko and was thoroughly in
agreement with his plan about encouraging the arts
through special ways of drinking tea. He had the priest
design a teahouse for his garden, the Silver Pavilion,
in Kyoto. He found that even his soldiers seemed to get
some mysterious satisfaction from looking quietly at
beautiful things, and drinking tea from splendid bowls.
It was in the next century that Hideyoshi invited every-
body to his great ten-day tea party.

The ceremony of tea drinking grew more and more
complicated as time passed. Rituals, procedures, and
formalities grew up around it. It took two or three
hours.

It is hard to believe that anything so seemingly un-
important as the way formal tea is served could have
as much influence on a country's art as it had in Japan.
It has affected ceramics, brought in architectural
changes, created a need and use for miniature gardens,

and has affected painting, as we shall see. Styles in literature and court dress also have reflected the refinements of the tea ceremony.

While separate teahouses became part of Zen Buddhist centers and often of great castle gardens, the tea ceremony also introduced the tearoom or the tea alcove as part of the private home where there was not space for a separate teahouse. This form of private tearoom was probably first constructed as a part of the villa of Shogun Yoshimasa. Yoshimasa's teahouse, Togudo, was originally part of his Silver Pavilion. This small, attached house, with sleeping room and a tearoom of its own, introduced the idea of a special place for the tea ceremony within the home. The new style in house planning, called *shoin-dzukuri*, which grew out of Togudo, includes a small room about nine feet square intended especially for tea drinking. Tea drinking had become a most exacting cult. The way the leaves were grown and prepared, where the water was drawn, how it was boiled, in what ways the kettle, bowls, and plates for cakes were arranged, the posture of those who took part, all were closely regulated. Utensils were revered, almost worshipped.

When we of the western hemisphere speak of having a cup of tea we think of something pleasant and refreshing. We visualize a comfortable teapot, warmed before the boiling water is poured over the waiting leaves, or a cup with a tea bag submerged in it, its familiar label hanging over the side. We expect sugar and cream, or lemon to be available. But such a picture has little to do with the Japanese tea ceremony which began so long ago and is still a highly respected procedure in Japan. There handle-less teacups or bowls, a tea caddy to hold finely powdered leaves, a bamboo whisk to whip up the tea in the water in each cup, and a bamboo spoon are important utensils. As each of the five seated guests sips the tea and passes the bowl on, he remarks on its beauty. In the same way each article that is used is passed around to be admired, and then is returned to the host. Details in the way all this is done of course vary in different places. Yet, although the tea ceremony became so stylized, and in some ways tiresome, perhaps no other practice has done so much to develop the sensitive side of the Japanese nature. It pointed to simplicity, restraint, and good taste after these qualities in native Shintoism had been almost submerged under influences from outside.

What lies behind ceremonial tea drinking for the Japanese is something important for all people. It is a search for the meaning of beauty in life, a search that each of us is making in his own way. Tea drinking was a time when close friends gathered in a place cut off from the routine of everyday life to meditate or discuss philosophy or beauty, to think of what mattered most— all things that might be impossible in the workaday world. The tearoom or the teahouse came to be a kind of sanctuary where people did not have to feel embarrassed to profess a love of beauty or to hold certain theories about life or history. Perhaps the greatest value of all was the fact that here they could be silent and yet not be misunderstood. One might say that behind the tea ceremony lay the same need that in the Western world is often met in a "bull session," except that it was turned in an artistic direction.

11

Painting, Oldest and Newest of the Arts

Long ago man pictured his first stories on the walls
of caves, and he tries to interpret himself in modern
art today. Because cave painting was often intended
to record events as well as to express feeling, it is
closely linked with writing. In the case of the Chinese
and the Japanese, writing often *is* painting, for their
original calligraphy is a skilled brush art. Watching

a calligrapher at work is like watching a painter. He makes careful strokes with a brush, and he thinks of form and space, darkness and light. Like a painter he hopes for a beautiful as well as a readable result.

We could list a number of things that are unique about Japanese painting. For one thing, it does not pay any attention to shadows. If you have tried to paint in a representational way, you will remember straining to keep in mind which direction the light was coming from so that the shadows you put in would fall at a reasonable angle. But the Japanese artist disregards them.

Overlooking shadows at once affects the way one feels about perspective. It can be overlooked, too, but it is the eye's habit to put it in in some form. So in Japanese painting one interprets the different horizontal levels on which various parts of a picture are constructed as perspective. In a play, we relate different episodes taking place in their own locations on the stage at the same time to each other—and just so we can bring the parts of a Japanese painting together. The action down front is the most important.

Another unique quality of Japanese painting is that the artist does not feel it necessary to fill in all the details. He includes the major ones and leaves the rest to one's imagination.

This leads to a third factor in his work. It is the value he puts on space. Space is not just the absence of anything; it is something present. A great Japanese artist once said that the most difficult part of a painting to execute was the space that was left unpainted.

Still another important aspect of Japanese painting is connected with landscapes. A Japanese artist will study a scene carefully and think about it and then go home and paint it from memory. In this way he will paint what is really important to him and not a photographic mass of details. He never seems to forget the decorative effect.

The Japanese artist is also interested in action. He loves crowds in motion and individuals doing something. His people are lively and high spirited, gay and frank. They are not set apart from the ordinary activities of living in cloud-enshrouded temples or on garden bridges, but stay in the street or field or on the shore, doing whatever they would be doing on any day of the year. Movement is suggested by using as few strokes as possible and wielding the brush swiftly. Yet a marvelous sense of pattern or design has made Japanese paintings a delight all over the world for centuries.

Until modern times Japanese painters have always been water color artists rather than oil painters.

Chinese ink, or India ink as it is called, is a mixture of lamp-black and glue. The hard stick of lamp-black is rubbed in as much water as is needed to produce the right shade. This is the basic water color paint. Other pigments, usually in powder form, are mixed as used and added from time to time. Silk or rice paper are the background materials for the work. Painting on other than paper screens or walls is usually done in lacquer or lacquer paint, which combines oil and lacquer. In these the background is frequently solid gold or silver.

The story of painting in Japan really begins with the coming of Buddhism in the sixth century A.D. The only earlier works found are wall paintings in tombs on the island of Kyushu. Some of these primitive pictures, which are thought to have symbolic meanings, are circles, dots, wheels, spirals, and triangles done in primary colors. Others are line drawings of horses or hunting scenes or people crossing water in boats. Though these last picture the life of the times, they may also refer to the afterlife.

Although the tradition of Japanese painting began with the arrival of Buddhism, only one sample of early Buddhist work remains, and that is the Tamamushi, or Beetle-Wing, Shrine, in the Horyuji at Nara. Iridescent beetle wings were once mounted in the honeysuckle design metal work that ornamented it, giving it its name. Paintings on the panels of the wooden shrine itself illustrate Buddhist stories. They are done with colored lacquer and are considered the oldest oil paintings of the world, since oil was mixed with lacquer in their execution. The pictures are delicate and have a feeling of flowing movement, as though the figures in them were airborne. Trees, plants, animals, and sacred persons are full of grace and rhythm. Even the mountains seem to move, and the arrangement of the characters in the stories and the suggestion of background depth or perspective, created by placing pine

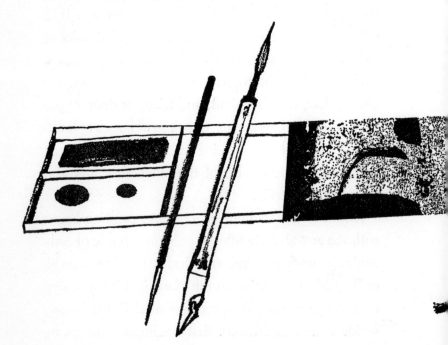

trees, bamboos, and willows at receding locations in the way described earlier, all imply motion. This work, which shows both Indian and Chinese origins, is very unlike the primitive wall paintings.

Three examples of Buddhist seventh century painting still exist. The first of these is at the Tachibana Shrine, also at Horyuji. The central sculptured figure of this shrine, Amida Buddha, has been mentioned in connection with sculpture. The nearly nude painted figures show strong Indian influence. Their languid eyes and the freedom of their postures in the arrangement show that the work did not come from a Chinese background, as much Japanese art had at this time. *Bodhisattvas* on the door panels, by contrast, seem more Chinese again. Different influences combined in this piece because there was still no clear Japanese style.

A second form of painting of this period is illustrated by the fresco in the temple where the Beetle-Wing Shrine is housed. This fresco has been compared with the well-known ones in the Ajanta Caves of India and also with the cave paintings of Tung Huang in Central Asia because the Indian touch is strong. The red, blue, yellow, and green shades of paint must have been put on white pottery clay walls. Four great Buddhas are represented, while eight *bodhisattvas* fill the smaller spaces, and flying figures known as *aparases*, or music-making Buddhist angels, and *arhats* or hermits appear on the head beams of the sanctuary.

The third pictorial representation of this period is not painting at all but embroidery. It is in Kanshuji and is called *Shaka (Buddha) Preaching at Vulture Peak*. It is intended to symbolize the idea that Buddha is forever teaching all who will come to him—in this case monks and ordinary people below him and angels and musicians above him. This work is particularly interesting because it has much less feeling of India about it than do the other paintings of the time.

A break in Buddhist influence in art came with a non-religious work. This is a portrait of the well-known Prince Shotoku and his sons. Probably painted in the second half of the seventh century, after his death, it must be a copy of an earlier work. It has great dignity, although it is not at all realistic. It is interesting not so much for its artistic quality as for the fact that it is probably the only early Japanese painted portrait in existence.

Still in the Buddhist tradition are Japan's oldest scrolls, or scroll paintings. These are the *Sutras of Past and Present Karma*, or *Kako Genzai Ingakyo*. The text is written just under the pictures, something like a modern comic strip. These scrolls were the beginning of a unique Japanese style of painting which tells a long story. They were unrolled horizontally as they were read or looked at, different parts of the story being separated from each other by some natural change in the scene itself, such as intervening trees or mountains. These *Sutra* scrolls of the eighth century have a fresh, primitive feeling and suggest by their style that they may have been copied from something even older. Human figures are too large for their backgrounds, colors are simple and clear; lines are very neat. Buddha appears over and over because these scrolls are about incidents in his life.

The single painting of the eighth century that attracts us most, even though it is hard to get a good photograph of it, is of the Hindu deity Kichijoten in the Yakushiji at Nara. In 767 the Empress Shotoku ordered that this goddess of happiness and beauty be worshiped in all provincial temples "to bring peace, timely rains, good crops, and happiness to the people." Although this little painting is only twenty-one inches high, it is delightful, and we can sympathize with the Empress's choice. This work makes us realize how hard it is to be sure how much of the painting of the Nara period was really Japanese, for in some ways it is quite Chinese. A good many of the best artists in Japan were naturalized Koreans who still had their Chinese manner, and who may have been given Japanese names. Ganjin, the famous blind Chinese monk, reached Japan in 753, and probably artists also came from China about this time. With the constant beautification of Nara, large numbers of decorators were engaged. These were likely to use Chinese techniques since the city itself was laid out on a Chinese plan.

During the hundred years between 794 and 894, painting became Japan's leading art, because the Buddhist sects that had become especially strong could explain themselves to their followers most easily in pictures. Philosophies and rituals were complicated; but pictures could arouse directly the emotions that the priests wanted their people to have. In addition, Chinese influences inspired landscape and figure painting. These were new, non-religious art. Kudara no Kawanari and Kose no Kanaoka, both of whom were scholarly nobles as well as artists, became masters in these new forms of secular art. The school of painting named for Kose no Kanaoka became so famous that in time many art works were signed with his name when they were really done by other people. He is best known for his scenes of ordinary life and for paintings of birds, animals, and flowers. Stories about his horses say that they were so real that they strayed away until he had painted harnesses on them! But the most important thing about this great artist is that his school of art no longer imitated the works of India and China. It became authentically Japanese.

Though the T'ang dynasty reached its end in 907, China's influence on her neighbors and the rest of the world was already immeasurable. Printing, the uses of paper, the famous Confucian system of civil service examinations, beautiful prose and poetry, and magnificent sculpture had spread out from China. She was truly the Middle Kingdom of the world's culture. Buddhism had been the carrier of that culture, as had trade, and had taken Indian and Indian-Greek as well as Indian-Persian touches with it wherever it went.

What was happening in the western world at this time? In Scandinavia it was the age of the Vikings; in Greece, Byzantine culture was at its height; in Egypt early Muslim culture was making itself felt; in Central America the first Mayan Empire moved toward the second.

In the year 898 the Japanese government decided to send no more embassies to China, but we know that unofficial contacts between the two countries continued, for traders and priests still went back and forth.

Buddhist influence on Japanese painting was still strong even in the eleventh century. A new sect, called the Pure Land Sect, represented Buddha as gentle and kind and called him Amida. He looks elegant, almost feminine. One of the most popular themes in painting was that of Amida and his attending saints coming down from heaven to welcome faithful followers on earth.

Another popular subject is Buddha's death scene. One of the most famous of these is the *Nehan* in Kongobuji at Koyasan. This is dated 1086. It shows how the expression on faces was depicted by this time. While the figure of the dying Buddha is perfectly calm and even the saints show no emotion, the disciples and *arhats* demonstrate their feeling at losing him, and the most grief stricken of all are the lion and his keeper in the foreground. Colors are cleverly used to emphasize the impression of the painting. Buddha and his saints are in gold, with outlines in red, but the other figures are in somber browns and grays and whites.

Landscapes of this time, which are to be found chiefly in the illustrations of books and in scrolls which portray interiors, with their decorative scrolls, show that a change has come. The bare, rugged mountains of Chinese art have been replaced by the rounded, tree covered hills of Japan. Soon landscape screens will have become truly Japanese.

But what are these illustrations and scrolls? Here

we come to one of the most interesting and most important developments in the story of Japanese painting: the Yamato-e narrative scrolls of the eleventh, twelfth, and thirteenth centuries. Although the narrative scroll idea was Chinese in origin, these were handled in a thoroughly Japanese way.

The earliest example of this school of painting that still exists is a series called *Shotoku Taishi Eden*, which shows scenes from the famous prince's life. They were first kept at Horyuji, and records say that they were painted in 1069. They are characteristic of the Yamato-e style, which uses such techniques as emphasis on decoration, a bird's eye view of a scene, and a single stroke representing both nose and eyes on a face.

Toba Sojo (1053–1140) painted a narrative scroll with a great deal of humor in it. He used animals to satirize all sorts of dignified and important people. Some authorities say that these animal caricatures were his protest against Buddhism, which was no longer respected as it had been. Toba's frogs certainly have a Buddha look, and a number of the other animals seem to parody the offices of priests and monks. He has suggested natural settings instead of really putting them in, while the movements of the animals are lively and engaging. Toba was a *sumi* or ink artist.

The Chinese tradition of ink painting had been

introduced to Japan during the Nara period. Copies of line drawings used to decorate the doors of the Kaidanin at the Buddhist Todaji in Nara are good examples. In a painting of two musicians, we find naked babies in the branches of the trees above them and the suggestion of a pleasant, lively atmosphere. The musician near the front has his back to the viewer instead of facing stiffly forward. But ink painting appeared for only a short while and disappeared until it became an important phase of Japanese painting at a later time.

By far the most famous of the narrative scrolls are the *Genji Monogatari e-makimono* by the artist Takayoshi. These illustrate the novel written by Lady Murasaki in the eleventh century. Takayoshi's style is very decorative, for the designs are simple and the colors are brilliant. He seems to be making up an ornamental design instead of illustrating the actions of living persons. Roofs are removed so that it is possible to watch the movements of people and animals indoors, from above. Instead of shading or true perspective he has set his figures on short horizontal lines to give an impression of where each one stands in relation to others. Nature is suggested by a lone tree or a single flower, for it is not important to this story of leisurely, refined life.

This period of painting when Japanese artists were beginning to free themselves of Chinese traditions holds even more surprises. We have mentioned two of them—the humor of animal caricatures, called *Toba-e* by a delighted Japanese public after their originator, and the decorativeness of illustrations for the story of Prince Genji. Here are some others.

Techniques that had been used for only religious paintings, such as sprinkling paintings with gold and silver dust or showering lotus petals down on praying ladies wearing elaborate court costumes, now became decorative styles for other subjects. Fans inscribed with quotations from the Buddhist *sutras* now sometimes glistened with mica. What is more astonishing is that beneath the colors of these fan paintings we can see that the original sketches look as if they had been put there by wood-block printing. Colors have been added by hand. So what we have are hand-colored block prints several centuries before they came to be one of the really important Japanese art forms. Small religious pictures of Buddha and his followers had been produced in large numbers by block printing for temple use before this, but these had not been colored.

Another example of escape from the past came in connection with popular legends. As we know these were often told and illustrated in the narrative scrolls, but there is something unusual in the one called *Legends of Mt. Shigi*. The speed of events in the story seems to be so important that the illustration is carried out in quick strokes of color wash rather than in the more usual heavy, decorative pictures. The same characters appear again and again in a sequence of episodes which remind one of homemade moving pictures. The narrative scroll technique had a great advantage because there were no boundaries between scenes, as in a moving picture. Small details often give an idea of what is ahead and build up anticipation. People in the story take on personality and act in character so that they are no longer symbols of an individual but the person himself.

This story about Mount Shigi is so long that it is told on three scrolls. The best-known one is called *Flying Storehouse*. It is about a famous monk, Myoren, who lived on Mount Shigi and who was said to have performed miracles. When a rich man comes to the temple and refuses to put any money into the monk's begging bowl, the bowl itself takes wing and gradually moves all the man's possessions from his storehouse to the temple. Mouth open, gesturing frantically, the rich man tries to halt the process, making every effort to follow his property. Line drawings provide a mood of liveliness, intensity, and then a hopeless slackening of excitement in a wonderful way. Even the landscape expresses the windblown haste of the racing, animated treasures. A story like this, told in painting, was so easy to understand that it could be appreciated not only by an artist or a nobleman or a scholar, but could delight any home audience. Its good points were pointed out again and again. It was reproduced so often and told so often that in time it became a fable.

Another splendid example of this kind of scroll is one eighty feet long, *Adventures of Kibi in China*. Kibi no Mabi was a real person of the eighth century who spent seventeen years in China and who gave lectures on that country at the Nara court. He is said to have helped create a simplified form of written Japanese. The artist, who was either Mitsunaga of the twelfth century or someone who copied his style, makes him into a kind of magician who uses the help of a ghost to confuse Chinese scholars in argument over the language in the palace at Nara. The ghost is, of course, Japanese, and the story offers all kinds of possibilities for showing the superior keenness of the Japanese mind compared with that of the Chinese, bringing in all sorts of humor and fast action. Drowsy grooms waiting outside the palace gates are delightfully realistic and funny.

When Zen Buddhist influence grew strong in the period of the military men in Kamakura, an architectural change affected painting. The alcove or *tokonoma* became a part of the house, and a vertical hanging scroll was needed. The beautiful horizontal scrolls, which had to be unrolled right to left so as to follow the story they told, gave way to a long panel or *kakemono*, which could be hung in an alcove. But this kind of a picture could not tell a story of many parts. Instead, it was something to suggest beauty or reflection. This was the spirit of the *tokonoma* which drew the eye as the artistic center of the room or the house.

Zen Buddhism appealed especially to the military men who influenced Japan for the hundred and fifty years of the Kamakura period. It greatly affected the culture of the times. Zen monasteries, which were austere with bare, clean courtyards instead of gardens that were beauty spots, were frugal compared with other temples and were suited to a disciplined, militaristic spirit. Zen Buddhism and Shintoism seemed to come together in their attitude toward nature.

This atmosphere encouraged realism in painting. One outstanding example is *Nachi Waterfall*. It was painted by a Zen monk of the thirteenth century and is considered one of the greatest landscape paintings of the world because it so well illustrates the connection between love of nature and religious reverence. The cascade seems to speak of eternal rhythm and unity.

Many narrative scrolls were produced during the Kamakura period, and hundreds of them are still in existence. Their subjects vary widely and include shrines and holy men, romances and battles, popular works of fiction and their illustrations, and religious subjects. As time passed almost every temple had scrolls that showed its origin and told its story, usually in a miraculous vein.

Tales of the Heiji Insurrection is a set of scrolls that deals with war between the rival Taira and Minamoto families before the setting up of Minamoto power in Kamakura. One of these scrolls, *Burning of the Sanjo,* describes the destruction of this palace which began the war in 1159. It is a fine composition showing fire and confusion with great dramatic power. The accent is on movement toward a definite goal; the semicircular formation of groups of people in action and the drawn bows and the moving wheels all add to a concentration of action. Billowing flames, terrified bullocks, and armed men make an agitated background for the central scene.

The most significant development in painting in the Kamakura period was connected with the quiet influence of Zen Buddhism. The introduction of the alcove and its effect and realism have already been mentioned. Masters of ink or monochrome painting and schools of painting were yet to come. Religion in Japan, which would never again influence art so much, now did so in this way.

Japan began official trade with China again after the Chinese Mongol dynasty fell and the new Ming dynasty began. A definite number of trade exchanges were arranged each year by Zen priests, since Japan's religion was now Zen Buddhism. Trade voyages between the two countries were often sponsored by temples, which used their profits for rebuilding and redecorating.

An ambitious Kyoto demanded luxuries that were signs of prestige, and the ordinary people wanted better things because times were good. Culture flourished as traders brought fine goods from China. Artists and poets took refuge in secluded temples, where they could work best. Sometimes great monasteries honoring the spirits of those who had perished in wars were established on lands won in battle, and became centers of the special art of ink painting.

Ink painting or *sumi*, copied from the Chinese style, had reached Japan during the Kamakura period. We connect it with the fine arts of flowers arrangement and the tea ceremony, which also came from Zen Buddhism. But this painting did not really become important until the fifteenth century, when it led all others. It is still used in freer ways by modern artists in the Kano school of art.

Brush writing is closely related to ink painting. The characters or ideograms of the Chinese written language, which were borrowed by the Japanese, have been described as pictures of things and ideas. Pronunciation was indicated by a "sound" part, or radical. Usually parts combining meaning and sound made up the word. But besides carrying factual meaning, these words could be things of beauty. The expert calligrapher was interested in form and design as well as in meaning. He wanted to achieve a satisfying artistic expression for himself, and he hoped that those who would see or use his work would also appreciate it. This way is very different from putting facts or ideas into words, as is usually done in alphabet languages. Spencerian script, which emphasizes the beauty of writing itself, can be thought of as being a little like the brush writing of the Far East; but the brush is much more expressive than even the finest quill pen.

The brush calligrapher of the past and of today is truly an expert artist. He has to be skilled in using shoulder, arm, wrist, and fingers in his work. His eye is trained to visualize how the vertical lines of writing will appear. If words are to decorate a fan along with other designs, the calligrapher-artist must choose suitable ones and an appropriate writing style.

The great ink painting of the past was also an exacting art. Lines made by an ink-filled brush had to be laid in the right relationship to other lines and to the whole composition, with heaviness or lightness suited to the subject and feeling of the work. The impression of swift movement or reluctant slowness, humor or poetic suggestion, boldness or delicacy might be called for. Rice paper and fine silk were the choice materials; but once the ink was applied to them it could not be erased, washed out, or covered over. It was there to stay. The way ink merged with the material on which the painting was done was a serious matter, too. Sometimes a pale wash had to be applied swiftly to cover the whole space without a stroke mark. When heavy ink was used, the brush might linger on its way so that the ink would purposely blend here and there with the moist background wash. Again, strokes had to be dashing and bold to delineate such subjects as a crouching tiger or an overhanging cliff of dark rocks netted with twisted roots. But nothing was left to chance.

It is easy to think of ink pictures as black and white, but this view is not correct. Ink paintings are monochromes which use one color in many shades. They depend upon the amount of water that is mixed with the stick, the overlap of layers of light shades on the paper, the speed with which the strokes are made, and how much the background absorbs. But what is harder to put into words about ink painting is the way other parts of the picture affect it. One cannot always be sure what shades different intensities will seem to take on. For example, a very pale gray may seem to be white when it is next to ebony; but it seems noticeably darker if it is adjacent to pure white. Gray may also pick up an imagined shadow because it is near a group of darker figures or trees. It may seem to be darker because it pictures a rising storm or wetter because it presents us with trees bending under heavy moisture. What this amounts to is that the eye adds to or subtracts from what is actually there through suggestion or contrast.

Ink painting can play other tricks. Where touches of color are put in, as they often are, in an otherwise black and white painting, they may be accentuated by washes of pure ink elsewhere which seem to borrow a touch of the color. I have in mind a scroll on which soft, green bamboo branches are seen mistily against a background of gray wash. That mist seems to be green until it is compared with pure ink grays, when it is clear that the mist is gray and that it has only taken on greenness to the eye, from the bamboos. One often has the experience of thinking that a gray is pinkish or blueish or greenish because of adjacent colors. The fact that the eye does this partly explains the marvelous appeal of the monochrome.

When ink painting became popular in the fourteenth and fifteenth centuries, it revolutionized all forms of painting for a time. The first works were strongly Buddhist. Many of the artists were, of course, Zen Buddhist monks, and they rather clung to the idea of setting a hermit against a landscape. But there was a practical reason for this compromise between religious work and purely representational art: there was still a great demand for paintings of holy men to replace the images that Zen Buddhists did not like. These paintings, which often included a Buddhist figure, were sometimes wonderful character studies rather than the earlier idealized images. They had simplicity and strength.

But landscape was the real field of ink painting. The Zen monk Josetsu, connected with Shokokuji, gave it a truly Japanese interpretation early in the fifteenth century. He lived and worked in a monastery near the capital. Only one painting that is unquestionably his is left, but many paintings bear his name because they used his style. A number of works by one of his famous pupils, Shubun, remain, although he was influenced by China a good deal.

Sesshu was the first to begin working in a truly Japanese water color style. He went to Kyoto as a boy and probably studied under Shubun. Later he went to China, enjoyed Chinese landscapes, and visited Zen monasteries in both the north and the south. He wanted to learn all he could from two of the great Chinese landscape artists, Hsia Kuei and Ma Yuan. He copied many Sung dynasty works because he liked them better than the contemporary Ming ones. Even though he used some Chinese themes when he returned to Japan, his touch was distinctly his own.

The single painting for which Sesshu is most famous is the landscape scroll in the Mori Collection in Yamaguchi. It is fifty feet long and portrays the changing seasons, beginning with spring. Its strong brushwork and sharp angles are typical of him. These qualities are also to be found in a well-known work called *Winter Landscape*. He sometimes followed what is called the splash-ink method, which is carried out by using a very wet brush and making free, splashing strokes. One may think at first that these are only blots, but on studying them one sees the images and ideas grow clear. This method seemed to illustrate the Zen principle of sudden enlightenment or understanding, which was supposed to come to one sometimes during meditation; suddenly one sees that a landscape made up of mountains, trees, houses, and people is really the universal religious spirit that lies behind everything.

Sesshu's works were beloved and copied all over Japan. His style affected many who followed him even in the sixteenth century; and although he belonged to what is called the Chinese school, he strengthened the newly born national style.

Kano Masanobu lived at the same time as Sesshu and like him is said to have studied under Shubun, although Kano Masanobu was a professional painter who belonged to the *samurai* or warrior class. It was his importance as a court painter that made him influential, rather than the quality of his work. The few examples that remain seem to lack the originality which Sesshu showed.

Masanobu's son, Kano Motonobu, was one of the great masters. He founded the Kano school, which is often referred to as the Chinese school of Japanese painting or the renaissance of Chinese art in Japan, of which Sesshu was the forerunner. But it is a mistake to refer to this school in such a limiting way. To the real student of painting, the style of the Kano school is much more than an imitation of the Sung painters of China. The Japanese artists tended toward a heavier outline and sharper detail, with much less attention to layers of perspective than is characteristic of the Chinese. Some critics have suggested that Japan's mist and rain and its poorer visibility made artists sharpen their work in an unconscious effort to make the pictures clearer. In somewhat the same way, decorators of painted screens that serve as interior walls in great buildings used heavy outlines and flat designs on gold and bright lacquered backgrounds to catch and reflect light, enlivening what would otherwise be a dull or even a dark room.

An interesting technique called line-emphasis was introduced by the Kano school. An artist employing this technique held his brush perpendicular to the paper in such a way that the ink took on the paper perfectly evenly at either edge of the stroke. If he could deepen the tone on either edge of the line by tipping his brush in that direction while moving it, it was to his credit. Such shading of the line stroke itself was called line-emphasis. This technique is illustrated in Motonobu's work by *Story of the Zen Monk, Hsiang-yen.* The picture is full of motion-swirling mists, sharp rock ledges, an active monk—all of which needed different kinds of lines and line emphasis.

Motonobu's grandson, Kano Eitoku, who lived from

1543 to 1590 A.D. brought a sweeping change to the whole field of painting. Instead of working on paper, he worked on walls or screens as large as five by twelve feet; instead of fine lines and composition suitable to limited space, large, bold designs leap to meet the eye with grandeur and brilliance.

Eitoku seemed to suggest the tremendous events and swift changes that took place both inside and outside Japan during the Momoyama period (1573–1615 A.D.) and is one of the greatest painters of that time and of all Japanese history. Though he was not born until a year or two after Portuguese traders arrived in the islands, bringing guns and ammunition, contacts with the western world revolutionized Japan during the fifty years of his life.

It was a stirring time in Western history, and the spirit of adventure and change reached the Far East. Queen Elizabeth and William Shakespeare lived, in England. Spanish ships reached North America. Christian missionaries like St. Francis Xavier crossed the seas to carry their message. Religion and trade battered at the doors of the Orient and asked to be admitted.

Japan, too, sent out traders and mercenary soldiers while pirates went on their own initiative to distant points. By 1600 there were few places in the Far East that they had not reached. When Japanese adventurers came back they brought stories which excited the imaginations of ordinary people, artists, and even the great military dictators of the period. Ieyasu, Hideyoshi, and Nobunaga demanded spectacular decorations for the castles they had built to be safe in with the coming of gunpowder arms. The Momoyama screens on the walls of their great halls presented dramas rather than pleasing pictures. We feel the strength in pine trees and the age that has bent and gnarled them. We almost draw back from the slim, weaving bamboos whose green stalks seem to engulf us. We have to check the thrills of excited delight that race down our spines when, suddenly, we *are* cherry trees standing in a grove, feeling the play of fragrant falling petals on our faces, hands, bare feet. Everything is lit with sunshine, for skies are bright blue, clouds are white, blossoms are pink, and tree trunks are shiny with shades of silvery gray.

Against backgrounds of solid gold or silver, tigers crouch, irises spring, waters gush, and twisted trees bend down to the earth and are softened by a tiny perched bird or an almost hidden cricket. Or one walks into a world of tall grasses and small wild flowers set against and mingled with golden clouds; or into a surprising historical event of Portuguese traders landing on Japanese shores.

In 1576 Kano Eitoku was asked to decorate Nobunaga's palace at Azuchi, the first of the great castles, and then Hideyoshi's at Osaka, as well as the Jurakudai in Kyoto. He sometimes used a huge straw brush to decorate walls and sliding screens and those that folded away. Not many examples of his work besides a famous *Hawk and Pine* screen are left. In this he emphasized flat space, bold design, and magnificent colors.

Another artist of the great screen period was Kaihoku-Yusho, who is said to have been a pupil of Kano Motonobu. He probably helped Eitoku decorate the walls of the Jurakudai. He painted a most unusual set of screens of fishnets, combining the colors of the sea with light green reeds in the foreground and pastel shades of the nets.

Other painters with their own characteristics followed. Chokuan-I was especially famous for his pictures of fowls. He liked to paint them with a very stiff brush. His son painted only falcons. Horses were also a favorite subject during the days of the dictators, but to the western student it seems odd that they were usually stable horses standing or lying in various attitudes instead of galloping horses with manes flying which are so beloved by artists in many countries.

When Hideyoshi banned all contact with the outside world, the outside world did not lessen its interest in his islands. Western culture was waiting at Japan's door all during the period of isolation, but she held out firmly and encouraged her own nationalism. Painting stressed traditional forms. The best known painter was Tanyu, a grandson of Kano Eitoku, who was invited to Tokyo to become a court painter. Through him and his descendants the Kano school continued until the Restoration in 1868 A.D.

Koetsu, who was born in 1558 A.D., founded a decorative school based on the style of the narrative scrolls of the Heian period. He was a great calligrapher as well as a potter and a lacquer worker, as we already know. Now we meet him as a splendid painter. Sotatsu and Korin, two other distinguished painters of his time, were also influenced by narrative scrolls. Sometimes they worked together combining beautiful writing with floral and animal designs in flat washes on their horizontal works. Sotatsu's six-fold screen illustrating scenes from *The Tale of Genji*, which is thought of as his greatest work, has rhythm and movement as well as bright and satisfying colors.

But the period of which we are speaking became famous in the western world when doors were opened again, because of an entirely different form of painting. This was *ukiyo-e*, or popular genre painting. It was painting of everyday life. Scrolls of the Tosa school had already told about the doings of ordinary people, and some Kano artists had tried what we think of as genre paintings, but they had been painted for rich people and had caricatured poor people. Now Japanese society was changing. Under military rule the merchants and ordinary townspeople had become richer and stronger, and they were looking for amusing art. Pictures of theaters and actors, of restaurants, pleasure places, wrestling booths, and all the people employed by them and entertained by them made good subjects. Though the capital was now Tokyo, the old capital at Kyoto provided endless inspiration.

Genre paintings paid no attention to traditions of the *samurai*, or to aristocracy. They presented whatever they liked and took delight in displaying the funny contradictions of life and ordinary events of everyday living like viewing the cherry blossoms in spring, or a family gathering under the autumn trees. Iwasa Matabei (1578–1650) is thought of as the founder of the Ukiyo-e school of painting.

12

Woodcuts, Miracle of Reproducing

We know that printing by using wood blocks reached Japan from China in connection with Buddhism. Woodcuts enclosed in tiny wooden pagodas were used as charms in many parts of Japan during the Nara period. Both the scripture quotation and the picture were sometimes reproduced by the wood-block method. By the twelfth century the scripture was often written on a block-printed background design.

In 1608 an ancient literary work, *Ise Monogatari,* appeared, illustrated with woodcuts. Koetsu, who was an artist with so many talents, is believed to have made the decorations for this story of court life. Other illustrated editions of classics quickly followed. Hishikawa Moronobu, another artist who painted genre pictures, is credited with really starting the great popularity of woodcuts. He realized that they would be inexpensive enough for ordinary people to own, whereas paintings would always be far too costly. So he began to illustrate current books with woodcuts and then to make picture books using them. After a time he and his pupils produced broadsheets as well as books. At first these were only black and white; but color was popular, and so was sometimes added by hand. Moronobu's themes dealt with great warriors, famous beauties, and having fun. Although color had not been added to woodcuts until Moronobu experimented with it, reproducing pictures or text in large quantity, even if only in black and white, was an astounding achievement. Before this every picture had been done by hand, a process much limited by the time it required. Now, suddenly, all the everyday people of Japan could enjoy art—and, even more surprising, they could see art about themselves.

It was a day when drama was so popular that it was almost a passion. This interest lent itself to postermaking. The artist Kiyonobu designed theatrical posters, first in Osaka and then in Tokyo, using wood blocks. He finally founded a school of actor portraiture and was immortalized by the Japanese people for it. A similar artist was Ando Kaigetsudo, who liked to make prints of stately women. These may have rivaled the pin-up girls of America in popularity, even though they were attractive in different ways. Five or six artists who followed his style closely came to be known as the Kaigetsudo Group at the beginning of the eighteenth century.

When Moronobu had first added color to black-and-white prints near the end of the seventeenth century, he had done it by painting in the sections of a picture by hand. After experimentation, a technique for using separate blocks for each color was worked out and used for two colors by the middle of the eighteenth century. A block for each color was carved from cherry wood. The location of where it belonged on the paper was judged by guide marks; a right angle at the lower right-hand corner and a straight line at the bottom of the left-hand corner. Even though only red and green were used for a long time, many designs were devised.

In 1764 Suzuki Haronobu, whose name was to become very famous, worked out ways of printing in more than ten colors, using a separate block for each one. He had an unusually keen sense of color and composition; but the fact that he was aware of the artistic importance of soft colors as well as bright ones made his works especially pleasing. He often created small pictures with extremely graceful figures with poetic charm. The field of his subjects was much broader than that of any woodcut artist up to his time. After his first multi-colored prints were completed, he was accepted as the master of colorprints. Haronobu died when he was only middle-aged; but during the last six years of his life, he produced more than five hundred prints of beautiful delicacy and harmonious colors. Among these is the delightful *Boy and Girl and Viewing Glass*, which is now in the Metropolitan Museum of Art in New York. In this print, the obviously imported peep-hole and mirror contraption that reflects the Tama River is secondary to the shy relationship between the boy and the girl suggested by their faces.

Utamaro, who lived during the last half of the eighteenth century, is considered the greatest master of figure design. He tended toward abstractness, omitting backgrounds and settings, and emphasizing the upper part of the body in his compositions. His lines are beautiful, though formal. His earlier works were picture books of insects and shells in which he carefully presented the actual colors and shapes from the point of view of a naturalist. These were not symbolic or suggestive pieces of work like some that were produced in China, but rather what would today be classed with flower and bird prints which are authentic representations. This same awareness of line and color appeared later in his prints of beautiful girls, his chief theme. He was very clever in preparing his outline block so that it could serve for both front and back views. The details which he filled in later differentiated them. He also thought of outlining faces, arms, and hands in pink so as to suggest flesh. Japanese women had never been presented so well before; for girls, mothers and babies, and domestic scenes were his specialties.

Sharaku, another interesting printmaker, is thought to have first been an actor for the *Noh* dramas. His works are almost all portraits of actors. He made at least one hundred and thirty-six of them in connection with plays presented in one year's time, between 1794 and 1795. His touch is so harsh that it is almost cruel, and his faces are quite displeasing. His technique combines a grotesque face with a foreshortened figure so that the facial expression is accentuated by a glaring background. He liked to use strong yellow, sometimes mixed with mica, in his backgrounds. Such works contrast strongly with other well-loved prints. Some people consider them caricatures; others say that Sharaku was depicting actors playing highly emotional parts.

At last, when it seemed that the age of great color prints had passed its peak and was about to settle into a monotonous repetition of itself, a sudden change came with the first of two great landscapists, Katsushika Hokusai. Hokusai, who was born in 1760 and lived to be ninety years old, used many names and did not choose this one until 1798. At the same time he began signing his works "Kako," too. The son of a mirror maker, he worked in a woodship as a young boy and then was apprenticed to a wood engraver. When he was eighteen he studied *ukiyo-e* or genre prints under Katsukawa Shunsho. He did so well as a pupil that after a time he was allowed to sign his work with a variation of his master's name, "Shunro."

Hokusai made more than thirty-five thousand woodcuts. They included ones based on the life of common people as well as landscapes. He started with actor prints; then beautiful girls and ghosts became his specialties. As time went on he signed each style of his work with a different name so that he came to have more than twenty altogether. In 1798 he made a set of small prints called *Eight Views of Edo* in a half western style. Twenty or so years later he finished his widely loved *Thirty-Six Views of Fuji*. Perhaps the most famous of all his prints is the one in this series called *The Wave*, in which one sees small, struggling rowboats in the trough of a towering wave, under the curve of which Mount Fuji can be glimpsed far in the distance, for once microscopic by comparison.

Hokusai was able to present the national landscape as a background for his own people with all their life and vigor, humor and pathos. The people of Japan were enchanted; before long the people of the world were enchanted as well. His works suggests the candid camera shot of modern times, for life is presented as it is, without apologies.

When he was seventy-five, Hokusai said of himself in words often quoted:

Since the age of six I have had the habit of drawing the forms of objects. Although from about fifty I have often published my pictorial works, before the seventieth year, none is of much value. At the age of seventy-three I was about able to fathom slightly the structure of birds, animals, insects, and fish, the growth of grasses and trees. Thus perhaps at eighty my art may *improve greatly; at ninety it may reach real depth, and at one hundred it may become divinely inspired. At one hundred and ten every dot and stroke may be as if living. I hope that all good men of great age will feel that what I have said is not absurd.**

Ando Hiroshige, who like Hokusai used many names, the second of the great landscape print-makers, has sometimes been called the successor to Hokusai. This is true only in the sense that he followed Hokusai in time. Many people believe that his works surpass those of the earlier artist. Because Hokusai did not produce his greatest works until late in his life, as he himself realized, his famous views of Mount Fuji were not completed until Hiroshige was in his prime. This means that in terms of their work the two men were really contemporary. They had become business rivals before Hokusai died.

The idea of the landscape print had its origin in the ink paintings Sesshu had made nearly four hundred years earlier. Since Sesshu certainly looked to the T'ang and Sung artists for his techniques, even though his work was clearly Japanese in feeling, we can see

* As translated by Kojiro Tomito and quoted in "Art and Architecture of Japan," Robert Treat Paine and Alexander Soper, Penguin Books, 1955, pg. 153.

that the landscape prints sprang from an ancient heritage. Some authorities feel that one may see both Chinese and Japanese elements in the work of Hokusai and Hiroshige; the grandeur and starkness of Hokusai falls in line with the dignity of the Chinese style, and the softness and humanity of Hiroshige's follows Japanese tastes.

As a boy, Hiroshige liked to make miniature landscapes of stones and sand. When he started to draw, he showed real ability. He studied under a friend who belonged to the Kano school. Later, two other artists helped him, and he also picked up some techniques from Dutch artists so that he became acquainted with several ways of working. Yet when he began to produce the sets of landscapes which made him famous, he displayed his own style. It was realistic, soft, moody, and beautiful. He is unique in his emphasis on weather. It is interesting to guess at possible reasons for his awareness of weather conditions. Perhaps we ought to begin with waterfalls, which suggest water and spray, as well as mist under certain conditions. We know that waterfalls have long been a favorite theme of artists in the Far East.

Fondness for mist and rain is hard to find in European art. Perhaps Westerners connect rainy weather with discomfort. In European landscapes, the general tradition seems to be that the earth is the source from which man takes what he needs and it is best seen under cheerful skies or against glowing sunsets, with an occasional storm for contrast. In Chinese or Japanese landscapes, man accepts what nature offers, wind, rain, mist, or snow, and goes on with his day's work, taking the weather as it comes. He carries on as part of the universe, rather than as a mite trying to subdue or master it.

Hiroshige expresses this spirit of acceptance, yet it must have been more than acceptance to make him so sensitive to the moods of weather. His ability to catch the feeling of mist, of snow-filled air, of the weight of snow, or the rhythm of rain *geta* on cobbled village streets as people hurry to finish their errands under an inky sky is simply uncanny. Again, the beating raindrops seem sharp, and one almost shrinks from their sting as they fall on the bare backs of laborers. On the other hand, Hiroshige's mists are so soft that they are almost smothering. They veil everything and make it unreal, distant though near, beautiful though actually soiled and worn.

Hiroshige's first great work, completed in 1831, was *Famous Views of the Eastern Capital*; his most highly praised the 1833 presentation of *Fifty-three Stages of the Tokaido*. He made many versions of this theme through the years, yet this first one which was printed by the Hoei-do shop seems to be considered the best one. But Hiroshige made many outstanding and beloved series of landscapes, and splendid bird and flower prints.

As he grew older, the great artist's standards of work declined. At heart he was always a painter, and thinking of his finished works in terms of the complete picture, he had to trust that the chisel of the wood-block cutter and the color sense of the printer would be authentic. The surprising thing is that while so many of the late Hiroshige prints were poorly reproduced, sometimes as many as ten thousand copies being made from one set of blocks, they could still be as passionately loved as they were.

When Hiroshige was dying, he composed these few lines, for which he has become famous:

I leave my brush at Azuma,
I go to the land of the West on a journey
*To view the famous sights there.**

---

* As translated by Y. Noguchi in HIROSHIGE, London, 1940,
Or, "I leave my brush in the East
  And set forth on my journey.
I shall see the famous places in the Western Land."
As quoted in Vol. 3, Kodansha Library of Japanese Art, Charles E. Tuttle, Rutland, Vermont, 1958.

Hiroshige had become a Buddhist in his old age and so it was natural for him to speak with longing of the land of the West, the Buddhist Paradise.

Color prints, which were so abundant in the seventeenth and eighteenth centuries in Japan, had an enormous effect in Europe when trade with the outer world began again in 1853. The first prints probably arrived in the West through the Dutch trading post near Nagasaki, while Japan's doors were still officially closed. But when trade was pronounced open, French artists were so excited about the prints that were now on the market in Porte Chinoise, a Paris shop, that there was an enormous demand for them. By now the first stages of color print making had already passed, and fine ones were appreciated in Japan as they soon would be all over the world.

These prints had a lasting effect on French art, for they encouraged the trend toward impressionism that was just being pioneered by Manet, Degas, and Monet. Toulouse-Lautrec also felt the influence of Japan. Collectors of Japanese color prints in England, Europe, and America were soon in hot competition for the beauties that came from Japan.

Today Shiko Munataka is known for his prints as well as for other forms of art. A Zen Buddhist, he likes many religious subjects; but instead of having the restraint and formality of the older pieces, his prints are full of originality. Even though he uses many traditional designs, they take on new life in his hands. He has made a large number of woodcuts and has illustrated books. He is thought of as the greatest of modern artists in this field.

13

Literature, Formal and Informal

Even though Japan had no written literature before
Chinese characters made it possible, poems and stories
had been handed down from one generation to the
next. These were a great oral literature. Special chron-
iclers connected with the imperial court were respon-
sible for keeping the national records complete.

In 285 A.D. a Korean messenger named Achiki arrived in Japan with Wani, a man who was a scholar in the Chinese classics. Wani stayed at the Japanese court in Yamato as a teacher. His descendants carried on the same work and were joined by other scholars from China and Korea as the years passed.

When Buddhism arrived in the sixth century, interest in learning grew rapidly. China became the cultural ideal of all Japan; and her literature, as well as her works of art, was enthusiastically studied and copied. The T'ang dynasty was at its height, and envoys and students came and went at the Chinese court, delighted with all they saw and learned. Schools for the study of the Chinese language and literature were started in many places in Japan, for it was fashionable to know Chinese. Scholarship depended upon the ability to write essays or to compose poetry in that language, since there was still no way of writing in Japanese. Chinese characters had the added prestige of being a classical language.

Oral traditions that had been preserved for such a long time were the first Japanese histories to be recorded, and they were written in Chinese. The titles include *Koijiki,* or *Records of Ancient Matters,* 712 A.D., and volumes on geography and genealogy. *Nihonji* is a book of chronicles which is also written in Chinese. Its date is 720 A.D.

The first books to be written in Chinese characters used only phonetically were Shinto prayers that may have been written down in this way even a little before this, in the seventh century. In these the written words have no connection with their original Chinese meanings but are used only for their sounds.

Another step toward creating a Japanese written language is found in the book of poems *Manyoshu, Collection of Myriad Leaves,* which was compiled sometime after 759 A.D. It contains over 4,500 poems by more than six hundred different poets. *Waka,* a poetic form that originated with folk songs, is used in these poems. Though the poems are written in Chinese characters used phonetically as in the case of the Shinto prayers, they also avoid word sounds that come from Chinese origins. The *waka* is made up of five- and seven-syllable lines which have no rhyme or accent. One form of *waka* is the *tanka* which has five lines of 5, 7, 5, 7 and 7 syllables, totalling 31. Another form, the *choka,* is a succession of pairs of five-syllable and seven-syllable lines which also ends with an extra seven-syllable line.

Manyoshu poems are simple and beautiful. They are about many subjects and suggest a young nation that is just awakening. Even today these poems are thought of as a great achievement of the Japanese people. When the court began to collect poetry it became an official undertaking, and the result was quite different. *Kaifuso* is such a collection which was being made at about the same time that the *Manyoshu* poems were brought together. The *Kaifuso* poems are in Chinese by Japanese poets.

A great change took place in literature between the eighth and the twelfth centuries, when the Fujiwara ruled. This came through the invention of an alphabet based on the forty-seven sounds of the Japanese spoken language written in simplified Chinese symbols. This system was not worked out easily. For a time one group would write in one simplified form, and another would use another. Some individuals even had their own private systems. Two main sets of abbreviated writing finally developed. They were originally based on two separate styles of written Chinese, but they came to be known as *katakana* and *hiragana*. Although Kibi no Mabi, whom you remember from *Kibi's Adventures in China*, is supposed to have had a great deal to do with the development of these styles of writing, not many of their symbols are to be found in his writing.

Although such shortened forms of writing were not standardized until the nineteenth century, they were important to Japanese literature long before that. The new step inspired Japanese creativity. Many who before had been held back by the difficulty of writing now found that it was possible to express themselves. Poetry took on new importance in the general literary awakening. The *waka* was again in use because complicated court life with its intrigues and love affairs could be suitably described by using it. The emperor authorized anthologies of the new works that appeared. *Kokinshu,* which was completed in 905 A.D., is considered the best of these. If a man was good at writing verses he almost automatically belonged to the aristocracy; he could be practically sure of a political appointment.

While poetry was flourishing, prose had begun to progress also. The earliest existing prose story is *Taketori Monogatari, Tale of the Bamboo Cutter,* a real fairy tale. One day the old woodcutter, Taketori, discovers a beautiful little maiden three inches high in the joint of a piece of bamboo. He takes her home, adopts her as his daughter, and names her Shining Damsel. When she grows up she has a number of suitors and assigns each one a task, promising to marry the one who succeeds. When none of them does, a flying chariot takes her away.

Travel accounts and journals became popular in the middle of the tenth century. One of the earliest journals is *Tosa Nikki,* written by a man who pretended to be a woman. Women did begin to write in diary form and in fiction. Their works became so great in volume and were so well done that they surpassed what men were producing. In the history of no other country has its greatest literature been attributed to women authors.

The greatest early prose work is *Genji Monogatari, Tale of Genji* (1010 A.D.), a novel by Murasaki Shikibu. The author was the widow of a nobleman, who served as a lady-in-waiting to the emperor's consort. This long book is the story of a fictitious prince and his romances at court. It is thought of as the first important novel written anywhere in the world. Its English translation has been quoted earlier in this book to describe court dress, and its illustrations have been mentioned in connection with painting.

Makura no Soshi, Pillow Book of Sei Shonagon, which was written about 1015 A.D., is very famous because it so clearly presents the intricacies of court life. It is not a story but a kind of miscellany of notes and opinions about the times. The author, Sei Shonagon, was another well-known woman writer of the period.

During the Middle Ages of Japanese history, 1192 to 1603 A.D., political unrest and the fact that Japan was divided by warring factions discouraged literature. Poets were likely to produce lifeless works using artificial forms. But one poetic form which began in the fifteenth century was to have an interesting future in the seventeenth century. It involved two or more poets who wrote alternating lines or couplets called the linked-verse-sequence. The first group of three lines broke away after a time and became independent as *haiku*, or *hokku*, a short poem of seventeen syllables. The lines were made up of five-syllable, seven-syllable, and five-syllable ones, totalling seventeen.

When Japan closed her doors to the outside world during the Tokugawa rule (1603–1868 A.D.) and began to unify as a nation, literature as well as other arts showed new development. Literature became better in quality and increased in volume. Many writers were now members of the military and merchant classes. They were free from any pressures and could write as they wished. Printing was used, and the number of people who could read was growing rapidly. The *tanka* form, which had first been connected with the ancient *Manyoshu*, was again popular. Now its short lines described life and beauty rather than the stylized ideas of the past. The *haiku* was especially popular during the Tokugawa period, for it presented the ideas of nobles and scholars as well as the beautiful themes of ordinary life in a terse, satisfying way. Matsuo Basho (1644–1694) is thought the greatest *haiku* master. Some of his most popular works are travel accounts interspersed with bits of poetry. *The Narrow Road of Oku* is one of the best known and most loved pieces of his writing. Basho was able to make the least significant object or incident in life something in which he and his readers shared a deep sense of beauty. So the story goes, he climbed to the Atami Pass in the Hakone Mountains to get a view of Mount Fuji on a winter's day, found the clouds hiding the peak from him, and wrote:

> *A day when Fuji is unseen*
> *Veiled in misty winter shower—*
> *That day, too, is a joy.**

The *Noh* plays are the oldest dramatic form of Japan. They began in the early period of Zen Buddhism, although the sacred dances from which they came are thought to be even older. Chinese and Indian stories were used in some of the *Noh* plays. In the fifteenth century Shogun Yoshimasa patronized two skillful dramatists, Kan-nami Kiyotsugu and his son Se-ami Motokiyo, and encouraged them to perfect

---

* Fosco Maraini, *Meeting with Japan*, Viking Press, New York, 1960, p. 109.

the play form. They drew on many old sources such as rice planting songs and comic juggling acts and enriched the serious, historical background of the plays. They deepened what was beautiful and significant and contrasted it with the comedy of interlude performances. Probably these plays can be compared with opera better than with any other well-known drama form.

Noh is performed on a wooden stage, built above the ground, open on three sides and slightly slanted downward toward the front. There are extensions for singers and musicians, and actors appear from a passage connected with one of the extensions. Actual pine trees planted along this passage, or bridge, and pine trees and bamboos painted on the wooden wall which forms the background of the stage, suggest an historical connection with early performances in woods.

There are two hundred and fifty *Noh* pieces, or plays, classified into five groups according to the types of characters or the subjects presented. History is the main theme. It is told by various personages, or in conversational form, broken by interludes in the form of a dance, a group of ordinary folk who come on the stage to tell of some event, or by a silent dance carried through by a single actor. Music is usually only that of flutes and drums and the chorus is a small one.

Masks worn in the *Noh* plays are important, for they have long traditions and are carefully preserved along with the beautiful costumes. The main characters and their assistants wear the masks.

Chikamatsu Monzaemon (1653–1724 A.D.) is often called Japan's Shakespeare because of his dramatic works. He introduced a new kind of play named *jojuri* after a twelfth century princess. It is a puppet drama and one reason why it became popular was that bloody historical events could be presented in this form. Puppetry became very skillful with the use of such complicated movements as those of eye, tongue, and even finger joints. Chikamatsu is known as the master of *jojuri* drama.

The idea of puppetry came from China long before this and had been used for religious themes only. But Chikamatsu was quick to see that everyday life was full of drama. He had a gift for bringing out the weaknesses and strengths in his characters, yet he did not judge them. This understanding attitude won instant support from his audiences. His puppet shows suddenly became very popular and many small stages for them were erected.

Another man who added to the popularity of the puppet shows was Sawazumi Kengyo, a noted player of the *samisen*. He began to accompany the ballads that were used in connection with the plays and this delighted the people who came to see them.

Kabuki, a third type of play, largely replaced the puppet theater about 1730 A.D. To some extent it grew out of the historical *Noh* dramas, for as these became more aristocratic and solemn under the patronage of military society, *kabuki* gave ordinary people what they really wanted. The name means "leaning to one side" or "being playful," and we can see that such a title is suited to the way this kind of acting began.

A dancing girl at a Shinto shrine is said to have been the originator. One day this girl, whose name was Okuni, went to Kyoto, where, dressed in a monk's robe and tinkling tiny bells, she performed some sacred dances with a man partner. After a time he began to write farces for her to act out on a rough stage, which they built of stones in the dry bed of the Kamo River. A few other girls joined Okuni, and they presented these plays accompanied by a fife-and-drum orchestra. The performances became so popular that others joined the troupe, and they toured several cities. But in 1629 the court ruled that women were no longer to perform. From then on to the middle of the nineteenth century, men took female parts, and some of them became famous for their impersonations.

At first *kabuki* was ignored by people of social

standing or wealth; but their resistance was soon worn down and they, too, began patronizing it. *Kabuki* gradually became the national drama form. Stage music which accompanied the speeches of the actors was much improved when the *samisen* was added to the drums. Some *Noh* plays were even adapted to the *kabuki* stage as time went on.

Special *kabuki* theaters were very elaborate. Sometimes they were two or three stories high with finely appointed stages, boxes, and galleries. A revolving stage was used in some of them. The audience arrived in the morning and stayed all day, bringing lunches or buying them from convenient groceries or restaurants during the intermissions.

In recent years a new school of *kabuki* playwrights has developed. These men have tried to bring in a modern point of view and fresh techniques. Often the scene is feudal Japan; sometimes the subject is a political one; often Western dramatists are copied.

Popular literature, which included plays and poetry as well as fiction, had really begun with the Tokugawa period. *Haiku, jojuri,* and *kabuki* had developed in this historical age. Fiction grew swiftly in various forms. The first important novelist since the Heian times was Ihara Saikaku (1642–1693 A.D.) who wrote of love and financial intrigue. Ueda Akinari (1734–

1809 A.D.) liked to write about supernatural subjects. Takizawa Bakin, who lived a little later, liked to moralize in very lengthy stories. But there were other writers who wrote of serious subjects such as philosophy and history.

When Japan renewed its foreign contacts in 1853, the new ideas that rushed in were almost overwhelming. Some Japanese authors tried to become Westernized at once; others resisted all change; still others tried mixing the old with the new. Much of the beauty and delicacy of Japanese poetry seemed to have been lost, at first. Poems which before might have spoken lovingly of blossoming cherry trees, now used the noises of traffic as a theme, with the intention of being modern. Some poets experimented with free verse. Western poets were translated into Japanese so well that some of their work has come to be thought of as Japanese. English and, later, French and German literary works were hungrily studied by eager Japanese scholars and students in the new age. All the philosophical and social as well as artistic thinking of the Western world was available to Japan.

A vast amount of literature was produced and newspapers and modern novels both had an important part in politics. The Russo-Japanese War of 1904–05 and the terrible earthquake of 1923 that shook the islands severely also influenced Japanese literature. It became more than ever concerned with ordinary people and their hardships and joys. The most popular style of writing was free flowing and easy to read.

Another change came with the end of Word War II in 1945. The psychological effect of surrendering to an enemy was a theme that was written of in many ways. Even famous writers could not escape it. This was followed by interest in French literature, which reflected a search for the meaning of war and of life and death. It expressed a hope of understanding life, or at least of seeing it as it really was. Translations of Western writers were in great demand.

The Japanese people respect knowledge deeply. They honor great minds like that of the famous bacteriologist, H. Noguchi. Although their language is still such a difficult one, nearly everyone in Japan can read. Newspapers have enormous circulations. Magazine articles tend toward serious subjects, and they, too, have a large public. More than twenty thousand books are printed every year. People may browse all the way through a book at a bookstore, if they do not sit down. Students sometimes stand through their research! Tokyo is full of second-hand bookstores, and in them curious minds from all over the world may meet.

14

Festivals and Fun

Anyone who travels in Japan is struck by the large number of toys to be found wherever he goes. City streets are full of color and life, seeming to overflow with gay dolls, tops, miniature tea sets, paper toys, and music makers of every variety. Kites and flags; battledores and shuttle-cocks—a thousand things intrigue one's interest. Color is on every hand. If there is sadness, it is covered by smiles; if sombreness, it is disguised with brilliance.

Many Japanese toys, especially dolls, have an old connection with superstitions. We remember the staring clay dolls that were found in the prehistoric grave mounds of the Jomon people. A deity of the soil or the spirit of a local shrine, a sort of doll, was often housed in an ancient Shinto image. Sometimes ancestral deities were represented by dolls. Long ago a common practice was to set up a large straw doll wherever plague had struck, in the hope that the evil spirit that had brought the illness would be satisfied to inhabit that body and travel no further. In the same way, even today Japanese villagers sometimes set paper dolls afloat on a nearby stream or river to carry bad luck away. The line between dolls and idols is a very narrow one. Sometimes dolls represent fairy tales like our Cinderella dolls and the Little Tin Soldier. And of course traditional or *hina* dolls are used commonly today in connection with *Hina Matsuri*, the Dolls' Festival.

Kokeshi dolls from Miyagi Prefecture are especially popular. They probably originated as offerings for pilgrims to use at sacred shrines. They used to be made of unpainted wood and resembled the *haniwa* of the grave mounds, for they have large round heads which rest on cylindrical bodies. They suggest many feelings by their expressions, and this fact and their simplicity make them appealing to people today. Because they are so attractive, they are sold in many Japanese resorts, although the gay, decorative paint now used sometimes spoils some of their charm.

Closely related to *kokeshi* and coming from the same general region are little squared-off horses made of wood. They are traditionally good toys for children to play with since they are supposed to give them strength. These horses are connected with a legend about a general who was fighting the Eastern barbarians. He succeeded in being victorious because a priest named Enchin made him some small wooden horses which miraculously brought one hundred real horses to help him win his battle.

Although toys are likely to differ from place to place, what they stand for historically is usually quite similar. Toy tigers and lions symbolize valor; horses offer transportation to evil spirits and give strength; masks can fool the enemy or amuse or terrify to suit the situation. The famous Three Wise Monkeys, "Speak no Evil, Hear no Evil, See No Evil," are found over and over, made of clay or wood. Cats are connected with good luck, and the figure of a beckoning cat is a common decoration for a store. Dogs, on the other hand, are

especially suitable as an omen of good fortune for babies, and so toy dogs are often gifts for the newborn.

One could continue indefinitely describing Japanese toys, but they have become so familiar in many parts of the world that it is hardly necessary. They are ingenious, countless, and cheap. While they may sometimes seem incongruous or gaudy when seen in Europe or the United States, in their place of origin they are altogether suitable. Japan is one of the world's largest toy producers, and most of these toys are of folk background.

The Japanese word for festival, *matsuri*, has a magic appeal to the people of Japan. Almost any town or shrine has some kind of festival connected with it. Fire festivals, sea-blessing festivals, feudal festivals, rowing festivals, and many others total almost four hundred if one goes into the subject thoroughly. Masquerades and dances, lanterns and ancient costumes may crowd a modern street to celebrate a holiday.

Among the nearly countless festivals there seem to be nine major ones:

> New Year's Day—January 1
> Adulthood Day—January 15
> Spring Equinox Day—March 21
> Emperor's Birthday—April 29
> Constitution Memorial Day—May 3
> Children's Day, Boys' Day, now combined
>   with Doll Festival—May 5
> Autumnal Equinox Day—September 23
> Culture Day—November 3
> Labor Day—November 23

Older celebrations connected with the lunar calendar are still sometimes observed. These are popular family fête days which include Seven Herbs Day on January 7, when rice seasoned with early herbs is served. Peach Blossom Fête, which is the same as the old

Dolls' Festival, and Iris Fête, which is the old Boys' Day, are officially combined in Children's Day, but they continue to be celebrated by families. Star Festival on July 5 is connected with an ancient Chinese story that says the orbits of the Cowherd Star and the Weaver Star, which are located on opposite sides of the Milky Way, cross on this night of each year. The Festival of Souls, or the Lantern Festival, as it is also called, on July 14–16, observed especially by Buddhists, and the River Fête, which features boats lit with lanterns and fireworks, are other interesting traditional celebrations.

There are also many local festivals that are observed and understood within only a narrow radius. One example of a local occasion of this kind is the Fire Festival of Mt. Kurama near Kyoto. It memorializes a Buddhist temple founded by Kantei in 770. Although the original buildings burned down long ago, they have been rebuilt. On October 22 of every year, a torchlight procession of boys and young men takes part in a ceremony that probably began when boys were initiated into the adult group.

Modern times may greatly change many of the old patterns of Japanese life. This process seems to be going on swiftly today. But the Japanese have always been particularly fond of celebrations or of making a simple occasion into a festive one. We have already seen this in the way the small graces of family living are carried out and in the way Zen Buddhism contributed to it in making drinking tea, arranging flowers, landscaping one's garden, and even the way one built one's house a question of ceremony.

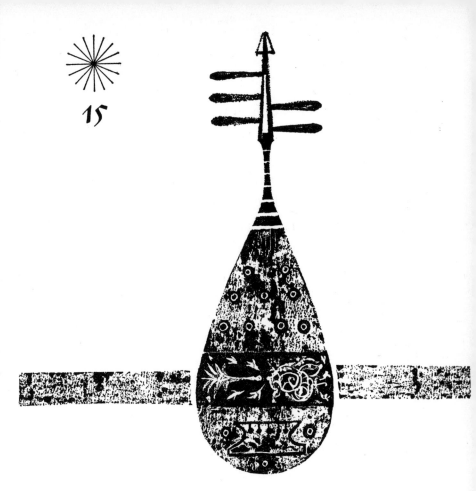

15

Music Merry and Mysterious

Old Japanese poetry from *Kojiki* and *Nihonji* was probably chanted or sung rather than simply recited. Three of these ancient poems are still sung at the imperial court and at certain Shinto shrines on special occasions. The way it is done is entirely different from the singing of modern songs. The existence of these archaic chants gives us an idea of the antiquity of music in Japan. From them we know that music has long been an important part of celebrations and ceremonies.

Probably the oldest instruments used by the Japanese were the *fue* or flute, the *koto*, which is a horizontal harp or zither, and the hand drum.

This early flute was a six-hole one which is still sometimes used in religious music. The later flute, *shakuhachi*, has a strange story. It came from India by way of China. In India it had five finger holes. When it reached China, another hole was added. To make the pitch right for the extra hole, the Japanese lengthened the flute. It had such a soft tone, however, that it did not combine well with other instruments, and after a time it was no longer used. In the thirteenth century someone lengthened it to one foot (*shaku*) and eight (*hachi*) inches. This is its length now. It is often used with the *koto* and *samisen* in interesting orchestrations.

The *koto* is said to have reached Japan from China, where it was brought in from countries to the west. The six strings were increased to thirteen, and it was improved in other ways so that it has become a favorite instrument in modern times.

Back in the fifth century the Japanese began to import music from Korea. The Korean harp or *kudara-koto,* an instrument that was held upright and played with both hands like the European harp, reached Japan at that time. In the seventh century Korean vocal music called *gi-gaku,* (not to be confused with *gagaku,* or court dances), was introduced. It is still used in connection with the lion and goblin dances, which are performed in some parts of Japan.

In the eighth century Indian music arrived with Buddhism, although no musical instruments came directly from India.

Meantime, between the seventh and ninth centuries, Chinese music was being adopted by Japan. The people liked it as they liked many forms of Chinese culture; but before much time had passed, they changed it to suit their own taste. Sometimes these adapted kinds of music were sung to the accompaniment of a small orchestra of strings, wind, and percussion instruments. Again, only a few wind instruments provided background for the solo parts.

One of the instruments that became especially popular was something like a mandolin. It is called *biwa* because it is shaped like a fruit of that name. Originally, it came from India, and it has a long and colorful history. Later in the thirteenth century it was especially used to accompany heroic ballads. A long time after that, in the late nineteenth century, a special type of *biwa* made in Fukuoka Prefecture, the *chikuzen biwa*, came to be thought of as a woman's instrument.

Two common kinds of drums, in addition to the old hand drums, were hanging drums, which were about four feet high and were used for festive occasions, and portable drums carried on a long pole by men who beat them as they walked. In addition there was a giant drum which was used only on court occasions.

Dancing usually went with music, and the dancers often wore masks with grotesque expressions. One form of dancing was *gagaku*, which has been mentioned before in describing masks as a form of sculpture. The word *gagaku* means noble or elegant music. It has been connected with the imperial court since it came from China during the T'ang dynasty. Even today *gagaku* musicians and dancers are descendants of Heian court musicians who have been carefully trained since they were children. Their music is slow and dignified. Each composition is a melody which is interpreted by eight kinds of instruments, three winds, three percussions, and two strings. The melody is played entirely from memory and since no two instruments play exactly the same part each instrument can be identified, even though there is only one tune being played.

When dance and music combine in the *gagaku*, it has a special name, *bugaku*. Symmetry, a limited number of movements, slowness, and stylized patterns are important and suggest ballet. Some splendid parts are those of running dancers who wear special robes and masks, and military dancers who are dressed in full military regalia and are also sometimes masked. What are now splendid costumes were, of course, at one time only customary court dress. The stages used to be the courtyard of a nobleman or a temple. Now they are built so as to be starkly simple. Audiences are usually made up chiefly of scholars and composers.

The first organ is thought to have been taken to Japan by St. Francis Xavier in 1549. Other missionaries introduced harpsichords, violins, and flutes. They began to teach Western music; but when they were banned from Japan, this was, of course, stopped for a time.

The *samisen* is probably the most common and the most popular of all Japanese instruments. Although it is generally thought of as being Japanese, it too seems to have come from somewhere else. Authorities say that it probably arrived from South China by way of the Ryukyu Islands in the sixteenth century, where it was improved by being made with the skin of a large variety of snake. The drum head was covered with this, and the strings strung over it. The name of the instrument comes from the Chinese words *san hsien,* which mean "three threads." As we have noted, the *samisen* provides the music for the *kabuki* theater.

When Japan opened her doors to the West after the period when she let no one from there in, military and naval bands brought in new kinds of music. From that time on the process of learning from the West affected music as it did other aspects of Japanese life.

Today opera, orchestra, and musicals all play important parts in Japanese entertainment. Japanese composers, producers, and directors of orchestras are becoming well known all over the world. At the same time, Japan is sending her artists to present her ancient drama and traditional music abroad. Though she may be demonstrating her ability to entertain according to the taste of the West, she also shows that she treasures her past. Watching the performance of modernized entertainers from Japan, one marvels that they can so well step out of their own culture and present another that they have had to learn.

Conclusion

To be alive and have meaning, music or any other form of art must be one's own. It must be sincere and genuine. Love of beauty is not a surface feeling, but one that lies very deep in human nature. For this reason the arts can unify the world's nations in a special way. In their arts people have always tried to express what meant most to them.

This experience of sharing through expressing one's self began when man first put a mark on the smooth rock wall of a cave, when he first held moist clay in his hands and shaped it with his fingers.

Down through the ages, in every country of the world, people have chiseled, molded, smelted, painted, woven, sung, danced, and written their ideas about the meaning of life—and have been delighted in the doing of it.

Today, Japanese products are to be found everywhere, and many of them are extremely beautiful. Although the Japanese touch is available in many commercial fields, the real gifts of the Japanese have not changed—a dauntless spirit and a *sensitivity to beauty*. The Japanese cannot escape either of these qualities. Though they may become more Western in their way of life, the world will always love them best for these two gifts.

The feeling of a mat woven of rushes, of a teacup shaped of clay and dipped in heavy glaze, of a lacquered box in shiny ebony, of a *kimono* splashed with autumn leaves, of unpainted wooden walls and delicate *shoji*, of a view of quiet figures absorbed in conversation beneath the ancient scroll and careful flower arrangement in a *tokonoma*, and of a garden just beyond—this feeling is as truly Japanese as ever.

Bibliography

Cox, Warren E.: *The Book of Pottery and Porcelain*. New York: Crown Publishers, 1953

Dilts, M. M.: *The Pageant of Japanese History*. London: Longmans, Green, 1947

Embree, John F.: *The Japanese* (pamphlet). Washington, D.C.: Smithsonian Institution, 1943

Encyclopaedia Britannica, 1959 edition

Grosset, René: *The Civilizations of the East*, Vol. IV. New York: Alfred A. Knopf, 1941

Hearn, Lafcadio: *Out of the East*. Leipzig: Bernard Tauchnitz, 1910

Japan Travel Bureau: *Japan: The Official Guide*. Tokyo: Japan Travel Bureau, 1958

Leach, Bernard: *A Potter in Japan*. London: Faber and Faber, 1960

Maraini, Fosco: *Meeting With Japan*. New York: The Viking Press, 1960

Munsterberg, Hugo: *The Arts of Japan: An Illustrated History*. Rutland, Vermont: Charles E. Tuttle, 1958
    The Folk Arts of Japan. Rutland, Vermont: Charles E. Tuttle, 1958

Paine, Robert Treat and Alexander Soper: *The Art and Architecture of Japan*. London: Penguin Books, 1955

Sansom, G. B.: *Japan, A Short Cultural History*. Cambridge: Harvard University Press, 1952

Tokyo National Museum Staff Editors: *Pageant of Japanese Art*. Tokyo, 1948

Warner, Langdon: *The Enduring Art of Japan*. Cambridge: Harvard University Press, 1952

Index

A NOTE ON THE TYPE

The text of this book is set in Electra, a Linotype face designed by W. A. Dwiggins. This face cannot be classified as either modern or old-style. It is not based on any historical model, nor does it echo any particular period or style. It avoids the extreme contrasts between thick and thin elements that mark most modern faces, and attempts to give a feeling of fluidity, power, and speed.

Typography and binding design by Atha Tehon.